Finding·God

Our Response to God's Gifts

*As I open this book, I open myself
to God's presence in my life.
When I allow God's grace to help me,
I see with truth, hear with forgiveness,
and act with kindness.
Thank you God, for your presence in my life.*

Barbara F. Campbell, M.Div., D.Min.

James P. Campbell, M.A., D.Min.

LOYOLA PRESS.
A JESUIT MINISTRY
Chicago

Imprimatur	In Conformity
In accordance with c. 827, permission to publish is granted on March 10, 2011 by Rev. Msgr. John F. Canary, Vicar General of the Archdiocese of Chicago. Permission to publish is an official declaration of ecclesiastical authority that the material is free from doctrinal and moral error. No legal responsibility is assumed by the grant of this permission.	The Subcommittee on the Catechism, United States Conference of Catholic Bishops, has found this catechetical text, copyright 2013, to be in conformity with the *Catechism of the Catholic Church*.

Finding God: Our Response to God's Gifts is an expression of the work of Loyola Press, a ministry of the Chicago-Detroit Province of the Society of Jesus.

Senior Consultants
Jane Regan, Ph.D.
Richard Hauser, S.J., Ph.D., S.T.L.
Robert Fabing, S.J., D.Min.

Advisors
Most Reverend Gordon D. Bennett, S.J., D.D.
George A. Aschenbrenner, S.J., S.T.L.
Paul H. Colloton, O.P., D.Min.
Eugene LaVerdiere, S.S.S., Ph.D., S.T.L.
Gerald Darring, M.A.
Thomas J. McGrath, M.A.

Catechetical Staff
Jeanette L. Graham, M.A.
Jean Hopman, O.S.U., M.A.
Joseph Paprocki, D.Min.

Grateful acknowledgment is given to authors, publishers, photographers, museums, and agents for permission to reprint the following copyrighted material; music credits where appropriate can be found at the bottom of each individual song. Every effort has been made to determine copyright owners. In the case of any omissions, the publisher will be pleased to make suitable acknowledgments in future editions. Acknowledgments continue on page 283.

Cover design: Loyola Press
Cover Illustration: Rafael López
Interior design: Loyola Press and Think Bookworks

ISBN-13: 978-0-8294-3170-4
ISBN-10: 0-8294-3170-5

LOYOLA PRESS.
A JESUIT MINISTRY

3441 N. Ashland Avenue
Chicago, Illinois 60657
(800) 621-1008

www.loyolapress.com
www.ignatianspirituality.com
www.other6.com

Webcrafters, Inc. / Madison, WI, USA / 08-11 / 1st Printing

Contents

GRADE 2

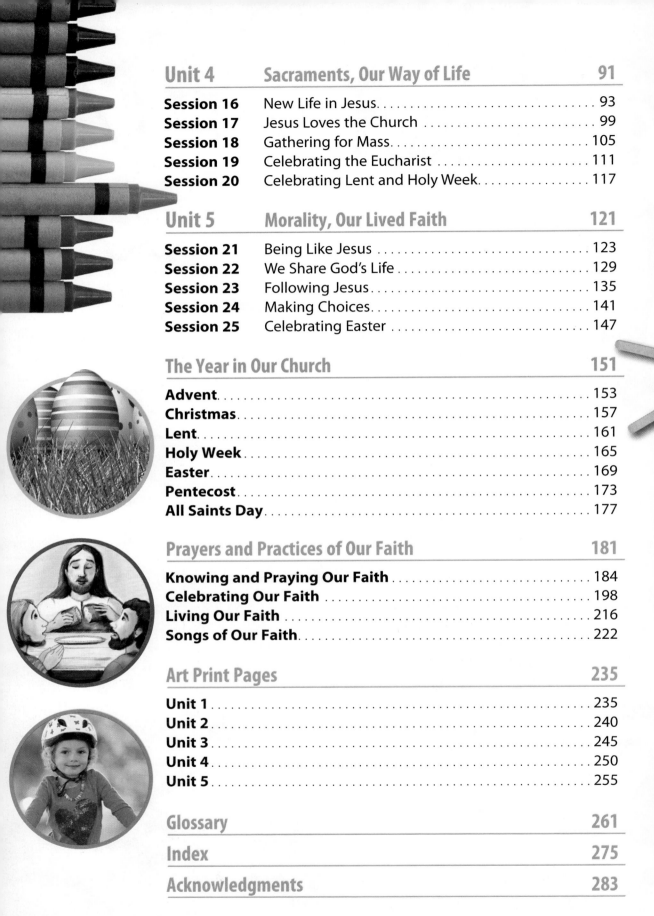

God, Our Creator and Father

Saint Isidore the Farmer

Saint Isidore the Farmer cared for the earth, plants, and animals. Although he was poor, Saint Isidore shared what he could with others.

Saint Isidore the Farmer

Saint Isidore lived in Spain. He and his wife, Saint Maria de la Cabeza, lived on a rich man's farm. Isidore worked for this man his whole life. He took care of the man's land with love. Isidore prayed while he worked.

Saint Isidore is the patron saint of farmers, farm animals, and farming communities. He is also the patron saint of picnics! We celebrate his feast day on May 15.

In many places farm animals and crops are blessed on Saint Isidore's feast day.

Have you ever made a card for a friend or a family member? Why did you make it? How did it make the person feel?

God Creates Us

Prayer

God, help me know that you make all things so that I can see how good and wonderful you are.

Our Loving God

God made the world and everything in it. Everything he creates is good.

God is Father, Son, and Holy Spirit. This is called the Trinity. God loves us and cares for us. That is why he always stays close to us.

Reading God's Word

Everything that God makes is good. We are thankful for all God has given us.   *adapted from 1 Timothy 4:4*

God's Blessings

People are the most important part of God's creation. God gave us the earth to live on, plants to eat, and animals to help us. God wants all people to love and care for one another and for the world he has created. God wants us to be **holy.** He shares his life and love with us. We can be holy because God loves us.

Caring for God's Creation

Think of a way you can care for God's creation. Then finish the sentence.

I can care for God's creation by _____

_____.

God wants all people to love and care for one another and for the world he has created.

Ready for the Sacraments

This year you will prepare to receive Holy Communion, the Sacrament of the **Eucharist**, for the first time. You will also get ready to celebrate the **Sacrament of Penance and Reconciliation.** As you learn about these special sacraments, remember God loves you and is always with you.

GO TO PAGE 235

Give Glory to God

God makes everything around us. We praise him with the Glory Be to the Father.

As you pray the Glory Be to the Father, think about how much God loves you and cares for you.

Glory Be to the Father

*Glory be to the Father,
and to the Son,
and to the Holy Spirit.
As it was in the beginning,
is now, and ever shall be,
world without end.
Amen.*

Think about the things for which we praise God. Thank God for creating you. Thank him for loving you.

Thanking God for Creation

Remember that God loves and cares for us and everything he creates. We give God glory for his creation.

God's Creation Shows His Love

Talk to God in your heart and thank him for his creation. Draw a picture of something that God created that shows his love.

No 2

Faith Summary

Because he loves us, God made many things. All of them are good. God wants us to take care of his creation.

Words I Learned

Eucharist
holy
Sacrament of Penance and Reconciliation

Ways of Being Like Jesus

Jesus loves us and everything that God makes. *Show love and kindness toward people, animals, and the earth.*

Prayer

Thank you, God, for all you have made. Help me love you by taking care of your creation.

With My Family

Activity Take a family walk at a park or nature preserve. Point out examples of God's creation. Pray a silent prayer of thanks for God's creation and for your time together.

Ready for the Sacraments Talk about the special sacraments you will receive this year.

Family Prayer *Dear God, bless our family as part of your creation. Help us care for one another and everything you create. Amen.*

Did you ever receive a special gift from a friend or family member? What made the gift special?

God Gives Us Jesus

Prayer

Dear God, help me always remember the gifts you have given me.

9

Most Precious Gift

God has given us many things. His most precious gift is his Son, Jesus. God gave Jesus to the whole world. Jesus wants to help us live good lives.

As God's Son who became man, Jesus saves us from our sins. He can help us live with God in Heaven one day.

Jesus is present among us in the **Blessed Sacrament.** The Blessed Sacrament is the name given to the Holy Eucharist after the **consecration** at Mass. In a special place near your church altar, you will see a **tabernacle.** This is where the Blessed Sacrament is kept after Mass. As a sign of our belief that Jesus is with us, we **genuflect** to honor the Blessed Sacrament inside the tabernacle.

We Genuflect

As Catholics we genuflect in church by lowering one knee to the ground and blessing ourselves with the Sign of the Cross. Who do we honor when we genuflect before the tabernacle?

_____

Ready for the Sacraments

Preparing to receive the Sacraments of the Eucharist and of Reconciliation is like getting ready to take an important trip. You do have to prepare, and the goal of the journey is to grow closer to God. The good news is that God is with you every step of the way.

GO TO PAGE 236

Jesus Is Born

Imagine you are with Joseph and Mary in the stable where Jesus was born.

You are holding Jesus carefully and gently, close to your heart. You know you can tell him whatever you would like. What do you whisper to him?

Jesus loves you. You listen with your heart to what he wants you to know. You are happy together.

Another Name

Jesus is also called **Emmanuel** and Savior. *Emmanuel* means "God with us." *Savior* means "one who saves."

Names for Jesus

Jesus is known by many names. Choose a word from the box to complete each meaning. The first one is done for you.

blessed   God   saves   with

Name and Meaning
Christ = _____blessed_____ by God
Emmanuel = God _____ us
Jesus = _____ saves
Savior = one who _____ us

Emmanuel

Faith Summary

Because of God's great love for us, he sent his Son to become man. Jesus is God's greatest gift to the world.

Words I Learned

Blessed Sacrament
consecration
Emmanuel
genuflect
Savior*
tabernacle

Ways of Being Like Jesus

Jesus came to show us God's love. *Do a kind deed for a friend today.*

Prayer

Thank you, God, for sending us Jesus. Please show me how to be more like him.

With My Family

Activity Make a thank-you card for a family member who has been like Jesus this week.

Ready for the Sacraments Make a Family Spirituality Time Line. List when family members received sacraments, as well as special moments when they felt God's grace.

Family Prayer *Dear God, we thank you for sending your Son, Jesus. Help us show kindness, love, and compassion, just as Jesus did. Amen.*

* This word is taught with the Art Print. See page 236.

Think about your family, your home, and the food you eat. In what ways does God take care of you?

God Is Our Father

Prayer

Dear Jesus, help me know and love God our Father as you do.

God Cares for Us

Jesus called God *Father* just as some children call their fathers *Dad*. Jesus reminds us that God is our Father too. God loves us and wants us to be happy. He wants the best for us.

God gives birds the food they need to live. Flowers grow strong and lovely with God's care.

Link to Liturgy

During Mass we stand to pray the Lord's Prayer. We pray this prayer together.

When we **petition** God in prayer, we ask him for what we need. We pray to God to help us.

We also **praise** God in our prayers. We tell him how wonderful he is.

God is our Creator and Father. We are his children. He cares for all people of the world because he is everyone's Father.

Jesus was a good Son. He listened to his Father. Jesus had trust in God. He reminds us to trust God too.

Ready for the Sacraments

We are able to receive the Sacraments of the Eucharist and of Reconciliation because we have been baptized. Through Baptism we belong to God's Church as children of God. Through all the sacraments, God shares his life with us.

GO TO PAGE 237

Jesus Teaches Us to Pray

In prayer we talk to and listen to God. Jesus gave us the words to the Lord's Prayer, or the Our Father. When we pray the Lord's Prayer, we praise God and ask him for what we need.

As you pray, keep in mind how much God our Father loves us.

Lord's Prayer

Our Father, who art in heaven,
hallowed be thy name;
thy kingdom come,
thy will be done
on earth as it is in heaven.
Give us this day our daily bread,
and forgive us our trespasses,
as we forgive those
    who trespass against us;
and lead us not into temptation,
but deliver us from evil.
Amen.

Praise Him, Praise Him

One way we can praise God and tell him our needs is by praying the Lord's Prayer.

Picture of Praise

Think about the prayers you have learned. Draw a picture of yourself praising God.

Faith Summary

Jesus helps us learn that God is our loving Father and is close to us. Jesus tells us to trust in God and place our cares in his hands.

Words I Learned

petition

praise

Ways of Being Like Jesus

Jesus was a good Son to God the Father. He trusted and obeyed his Father. *Listen to your parents and trust them with your cares.*

Prayer

Thank you, Jesus, for teaching me to trust in God and to place my cares in his hands.

With My Family

Activity As a family, take turns blindfolding and guiding one another around your house. Discuss similarities in trusting your guides and in trusting God.

Ready for the Sacraments Talk about your Baptism, including your godparents, the celebration, and how the people present welcomed you to your family and the family of God.

Family Prayer *Dear God, bless our family. Help us to trust in you always.*

We have received the gift of life. We celebrate it in many ways. How have you celebrated your gift of life lately?

God's Life for Us

Prayer

Dear God, bring me closer to your Holy Spirit so that I can remember he is always with me.

21

Simeon of Jerusalem

There was a man named Simeon who lived in Jerusalem.

Simeon loved God. He listened to the Holy Spirit. The Holy Spirit promised Simeon he would not die until he had seen the **Messiah.**

One day Simeon was in the **Temple,** where Jewish people worshiped God. Mary and Joseph came to the Temple. Simeon saw Mary carrying the baby Jesus.

Guided by the grace of the Holy Spirit, Simeon knew Jesus was the Savior.

Simeon took Jesus into his arms. He praised God and said, "Now, Master, you may let your servant go in peace. My eyes have seen the Savior. He is the one you have promised to all people."

adapted from Luke 2:25–32

Simeon

Did You Know?

The name *Simeon* means "God has heard."

The Holy Spirit

The Holy Spirit helps us know God is always with us. The Holy Spirit guides us, as he guided Simeon.

The Holy Spirit also gives us **faith** in God. By listening to the Holy Spirit, we learn to believe and trust in God. We learn to care for ourselves and others as God wants us to.

Learning to Care for Others

What is one way that you can care for others? Finish the sentence.

I can care for others by _____

_____

_____.

Ready for the Sacraments

Know God's grace is already working in you to help you prepare to receive the Sacraments of Reconciliation and of the Eucharist. This grace gives you the strength to do the right thing even when it is difficult. It gives you joy in friendship and a growing desire to love God more every day.

GO TO PAGE 238

Holy Spirit, Be Our Guide

The Holy Spirit is in your heart, waiting to guide you. Ask the Holy Spirit for help by praying this prayer.

Prayer to the Holy Spirit

> Come, Holy Spirit, fill the hearts of your faithful.
> And kindle in them the fire of your love.
> Send forth your Spirit and they shall be created.
> And you will renew the face of the earth.

Thank the Holy Spirit for being your guide and filling your heart with love.

Holy Spirit, Guide Me

Listen to the Holy Spirit in your heart. Trace three paths that show how the Holy Spirit guides you in the right direction.

Faith Summary

The Holy Spirit is present in our lives. When we listen to the Spirit, we recognize God in ordinary things.

Words I Learned

faith
Messiah
Temple

Ways of Being Like Jesus

Jesus knew that God is all around us in ordinary things. *Look for God in the world around you.*

Prayer

Holy Spirit, thank you for being my guide. Help me always listen to you and do what you want me to do.

With My Family

Activity Guided by the Holy Spirit, show goodness and love to others. Help neighbors in need by raking their leaves, bringing them a meal, making them cards, or visiting them.

Ready for the Sacraments As a family, share ways you feel God helping you at home, at work, at school, and at play.

Family Prayer *Dear God, help us to show goodness to one another. Help us to love others as you do. Amen.*

Celebrating Ordinary Time

The Church keeps a calendar to mark different seasons and special times in Jesus' life. Celebrating these seasons helps us think about God's love in our own lives.

Ordinary Time is celebrated two times during each liturgical year—from Christmas until Lent and from Easter until Advent.

Prayer

Dear Jesus, I want to grow closer to you during Ordinary Time. Help me to grow in your love.

Jesus Feeds Us

Ordinary Time is a time to be fed by Jesus Christ, the **Bread of Life.**

We are filled with grace each time we receive the Body and Blood of Christ at Mass.

How Can I Grow?

Put an X on the line to answer each question.

1. How can I grow in my knowledge of Jesus?

   _____ I can play with my friends.

   _____ I can pray and read my Bible.

2. How can I grow in my love for Jesus?

   _____ I can ride my bike around the block.

   _____ I can help someone who is sick or sad.

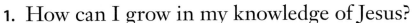

Reading God's Word

"I am the bread of life."

John 6:48

Mass During Ordinary Time

Watch as parish members process to Holy Communion. Are they joyful? Prayerful? Filled with peace? Think about how they might feel receiving Jesus in Holy Communion.

What We Experience

At Mass during Ordinary Time, the priest wears green vestments. Often the church is decorated with plants and flowers.

Color the picture green where it's dotted and fill in the rest of the picture with your choice of colors.

Ready for the Sacraments

Sacraments allow us to meet God as we are. They use ordinary objects or actions like water (for Baptism), bread (for the Eucharist), and a blessing (for Reconciliation) to show God wants to feed us, heal us, and free us from sin. We don't have to travel to the ends of the earth for such a great treasure. In the sacraments God comes to meet us and be with us.

GO TO PAGE 239

Faith Summary

Ordinary Time is celebrated two times during each liturgical year. It is a time to be fed by Jesus, the Bread of Life.

Words I Learned	**Ways of Being Like Jesus**
Bread of Life	Jesus loves and cares for everyone.
chasuble*	*Show kindness to everyone, especially when others are unkind.*

Prayer

Dear Jesus, thank you for the gift of your love in Holy Communion. Help me to love like you.

With My Family

Activity During Mass watch for the priest's green vestments. Talk about how the Church celebrates Ordinary Time.

Ready for the Sacraments Ask family members to draw crosses on sticky notes and place them where they feel God's presence in your home. Discuss these special places.

Family Prayer Invite your family to use Ordinary Time to grow in faith together by making a prayer journal for special prayer intentions or requests.

* This word is taught with the Art Print. See page 239.

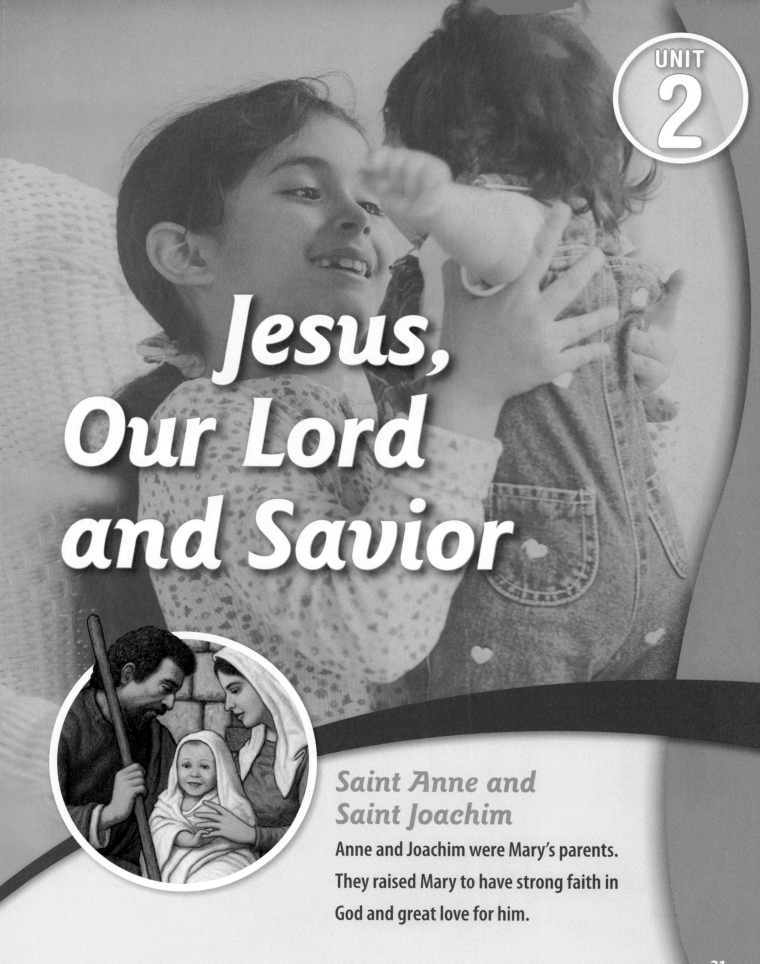

Jesus, Our Lord and Savior

Saint Anne and Saint Joachim

Anne and Joachim were Mary's parents. They raised Mary to have strong faith in God and great love for him.

Saint Anne and Saint Joachim

Mary was devoted to God. She listened to God and became the Mother of Jesus. She was open to God because of her faith and the faith of her parents, Anne and Joachim.

Saint Anne is the patron saint of mothers. She is also the patron saint of women who are expecting babies. Saint Joachim is the patron saint of fathers.

How do you obey your parents? What do you help them with?

Jesus Is Faithful

Prayer

Jesus, Son of God, give me the grace to love God and to be faithful to him.

God's Special Rules

Jesus, Mary, and Joseph were followers of the Jewish faith. They accepted the **Ten Commandments** as God's rules and obeyed them. As Catholics we also follow the Ten Commandments. We follow Jesus when we obey the Commandments.

First Commandment: I am your God; love nothing more than me.

I will worship you alone, God, above all other people and things.

Second Commandment: Use God's name with respect.

I will speak your name with respect only, never in anger or hate.

Third Commandment: Keep the Lord's Day holy.

I will go to church on Sundays and celebrate the Eucharist.

Fourth Commandment: Honor and obey your parents.

I will honor and obey my parents, grandparents, and teachers.

Fifth Commandment: Treat all human life with respect.

I will care for my life and the lives of other people. I will not harm myself or others.

be happy

Sixth Commandment: Respect married life.

I will pray for married people to treat each other lovingly.

Seventh Commandment: Respect what belongs to others.

I will not steal, cheat, or take things without permission.

Eighth Commandment: Tell the truth.

I will be honest and truthful. I will not lie.

Ninth Commandment: Respect your neighbors and your friends.

I will not talk about anyone in a mean way.
I will treat everyone as Jesus would.

Tenth Commandment: Be happy with what you have.

I will appreciate the gifts God has given me.
I will not be jealous of other people.

adapted from Exodus 20:1–17

Ready for the Sacraments

Jesus taught us by his example that we can trust God his Father. Even when he was most afraid, Jesus trusted that God his Father would always be there for him. Jesus said the same is true for us. God our Father loves us and will always care for us no matter where we go or what we do. He always forgives us and welcomes us back.

GO TO PAGE 240

Time with God

Jesus felt at home in the Temple. This was the special place where he could worship God the Father.

You have a special place where you can worship God the Father too. The next time you go to church, take time to be quiet before or after Mass. Make this your special time and place to be with God our Father. Imagine how happy he is to be with you!

Picture yourself in church. Thank God that you are his child. Be still with your heavenly Father.

Jesus the Good Son

Jesus knew he should obey his parents and not cause them to worry. That is why he did as they asked.

Like Jesus, you should listen to and obey your parents. Ask Jesus to help you obey them.

At Church

Use the words in the box to complete the sentences.

> Temple   obey   special   church

1. At _____ we pray to God.

2. Church is a _____ place where we can talk quietly with God.

3. We may ask God to help us _____ our parents and follow the Ten Commandments.

4. We pray to God in church just as Jesus did in the _____ .

Faith Summary

Jesus listened to God and followed the Ten Commandments. The Commandments help us love God and others.

Words I Learned

Ten Commandments

Ways of Being Like Jesus

Jesus honored his parents. *Honor your parents by obeying and helping them.*

Prayer

Thank you, God, for giving us your Commandments. Help me follow them as Jesus did.

With My Family

Activity Show love by passing it on. When a family member does something nice for you, do something nice for another family member.

Ready for the Sacraments We trust that our families are there for us. Have family members finish the sentence "I trust you because . . ." Thank God for your family.

Family Prayer Dear God, give our family the strength to follow your Commandments and love as you did.

What are some good things you have done for your family? What good things has your family done for you?

Jesus Saves Us

Prayer

Jesus, my friend, walk with me as I learn to follow your example of love and goodness.

Jesus Cares for Everybody

Jesus followed God, obeyed Mary and Joseph, and helped people in need. Jesus told people how much God loved them. Jesus had a special love for those who were sick. He showed God's love for them by healing them.

But some people became angry with Jesus. They put him to death on a cross.

When Jesus died on the cross, everybody thought it was the end of his life. But God raised Jesus from the dead.

Jesus Is Alive

Now Jesus is alive in Heaven. He is also with us, helping us and caring for us. He wants us to love others as he loves us.

Knowing Jesus' Love

How can you follow Jesus' example of love? How can you care for the people around you?

Write your ideas on the lines below.

_____

_____

_____

_____

_____

Ready for the Sacraments

When we have done something wrong or selfish, we might want to keep it a secret. Adam and Eve tried to hide from God after they disobeyed his wishes. But it is important to tell the truth to ourselves and to God. In the Sacrament of Reconciliation, we no longer hide from God.

GO TO PAGE 241

Helping People in Need

The stories of Jesus healing people who were sick show us that we should help people in need. Imagine how excited people must have been when Jesus healed them.

Now imagine you are close to people who need help. What would Jesus want you to do for them?

Silently pray to Jesus. Ask him to show you ways to care for those in need. Tell him how you will help someone in your family, church, school, or neighborhood.

Caring for Others

Jesus wants us to care for people in need. Like Jesus, we share God's love when we show kindness, offer help, or take time for others.

Below are stories about people in need. Write a **J** on the line that shows how you can care for others like Jesus.

1. A friend is caught in the rain with no umbrella.

   _____ Share your umbrella.

   _____ Turn your back and walk away.

2. Your father is fixing the front door at home.

   _____ Play video games.

   _____ Get tools for your father.

3. A friend does not understand the homework.

   _____ Explain the assignment to your friend.

   _____ Tell everybody your friend is going to fail.

4. A classmate gets hurt on the playground.

   _____ Pretend you don't notice.

   _____ Get help for your classmate.

Living My Faith

Faith Summary

Jesus is alive in Heaven. He is also with us.
He helps us love others.

Word I Learned

miracle*

Ways of Being Like Jesus

Jesus helped people in need.
*Look around you for others who might need help and lend
them a hand.*

Prayer

*Thank you, Jesus, for showing me your loving ways
so that I can share your love with others.*

With My Family

Activity Spend time visiting a local
retirement home together.

Ready for the Sacraments As a family, recall a
time you were traveling and got lost. How did
you feel when you were lost? What helped you
find your way again? How is this experience
like the Sacrament of Reconciliation?

Family Prayer *Dear God, help us grow more like
Jesus each day.*

* This word is taught with the Art Print. See page 241.

When have you been invited to a party? How did it feel to be included?

Jesus Calls Us to Love

Prayer

Loving Jesus, help me learn to follow you and care for people as you do.

45

Leaders of Our Church

The leaders of the Catholic Church care for their people. We look to these leaders to help us and guide us.

Our Pope

Peter was one of the first followers of Jesus. Peter knew that Jesus was the Messiah. Jesus chose Peter to become the leader of the Church.

Peter's role as the leader of the Church has been passed on through the years. Today the **pope** leads the Church as Peter did.

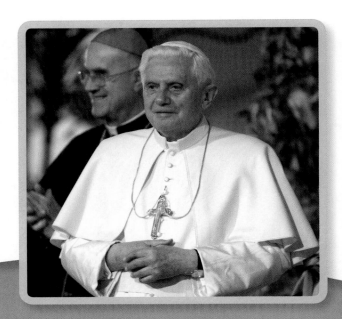

The pope lives at Vatican City near Rome, Italy.

Reading God's Word

Jesus traveled through Galilee. He taught people, shared God's message, and cured those who were sick.

adapted from Matthew 4:23

Our Bishops

A **bishop** cares for many parishes. He tends to the needs of Catholics who belong to those parishes. Each bishop carries a shepherd's staff called a **crosier.** The crosier reminds us that the bishop cares for his people. In this way the bishop is like Jesus, the Good Shepherd.

Ready for the Sacraments

We feel sad when we hurt people we love because we don't feel as close to them. When we sin, we feel sad because we feel far away from God. But he is always close and ready to forgive us.

GO TO PAGE 242

God Cares

Jesus tells us how much God loves and cares for us. Think about how we can share his love and his care with everybody we meet.

Think of people in your life who love you. Just as they love you, God too loves you and wants you to be happy. Think of some of the ways God has cared for you.

Now ask God to help you care for others as he cares for you. Tell him one way you will help another person.

Jesus' Invitation

You have received Jesus' invitation to be close to him. What is he inviting you to do? What is your response? Write it on the lines below.

Dear Jesus,

_____

_____

_____

_____

_____

_____

_____

Your friend,

_____

Invitation

Meet a Saint

Saint Martín de Porres spent his life helping others in Peru. Martín loved and cared for humans and animals. By caring for others, Martín followed Jesus.

Faith Summary

Jesus came to invite everyone to follow God. He chose Peter to lead the Church. We follow God by helping people in need.

Words I Learned

bishop
crosier
parable*
pope

Ways of Being Like Jesus

Jesus invites everyone to follow God. *Include others in work or play.*

Prayer

Thank you, Jesus, for showing me how much God loves me.

With My Family

Activity Ask your family to invite someone to dinner and make him or her feel welcome.

Ready for the Sacraments Ask family members to tell you about a time when someone forgave them. Ask them how they felt before asking for forgiveness and how they felt after saying "I'm sorry" and receiving forgiveness.

Family Prayer Dear God, guide us to follow you each day and to help those in need.

Think of a time you lost something. Where did you search for it? How did you feel when you found it?

Jesus Cares for Us

Prayer

Jesus, help me recognize all the ways God cares for me.

The Parable of the Lost Sheep

Jesus said, "Always remember that each person is important to God. An angel in heaven watches over each one of them."

Then Jesus told a parable that teaches an important lesson. "What do you think about this? A man has 100 sheep. If one of them gets lost, he will leave the other 99 and search for the one lost sheep."

"And if he finds the lost sheep, he is happier with it than he is with the other 99 sheep."

He teaches us, "That is also what our heavenly Father wants. He does not want one single person to be lost."

adapted from Matthew 18:10–14

one lost sheep

Reading God's Word

I am the good shepherd. A good shepherd lays down his life for the sheep.

John 10:11

Shepherding God's People

A priest serves the parish in many ways. He celebrates Mass daily, visits people who are sick, teaches, and helps people in need.

Deacons also serve the people in their parishes. They help the priests teach about God and lead the people in prayer. Religious sisters and brothers, teachers, and catechists also help people learn about God.

Ready for the Sacraments

Jesus told us he was like a good shepherd who took care of his sheep. If a sheep got lost, the shepherd would find the sheep again. Sometimes we make mistakes and even do bad things. We can lose our way. In the Sacrament of Reconciliation, Jesus is always ready to help us find our way again.

GO TO PAGE 243

The Good Shepherd

The Book of Psalms is a section of the Bible. Psalms are special songs or prayers. Psalm 23 praises God.

Lord, you are my shepherd,
  there is nothing that I need.

You make sure I have enough to eat,
  you see that I have good water to drink,
  you give me great strength.

You guide me along the right path,
  so that I may do as you wish.

Even when I am in danger,
  I am not afraid because you are with me,
  your care gives me courage.

adapted from Psalm 23

God is the Good Shepherd. He will always take care of you. Thank God for loving you so much.

God Is Our Shepherd

A good shepherd cares about every sheep, just as God cares for every one of us.

Find the Lost Sheep

Solve the maze to lead this shepherd to his lost sheep.

Faith Summary

Jesus teaches us about God's loving concern for us. The leaders of the Church help us to know and love God.

Word I Learned

deacon

Ways of Being Like Jesus

Jesus the Good Shepherd cares for all his sheep. *Take care of your friends and family.*

Prayer

Thank you, God, for being my Good Shepherd and for always staying by my side.

With My Family

Activity Plan a special day for someone in your family.

Ready for the Sacraments Say you're sorry without excuses or blame. God will always forgive us when we're sorry, so we no longer have to hide what we've done.

Family Prayer Dear God, *be with the pastors of the Church. Give them strength and guidance as they serve your people.*

Celebrating Advent

The Church's liturgical year begins with Advent. Advent is the season before Christmas. It begins four Sundays before December 25 and ends at Mass on Christmas Eve.

Prayer

Dear Jesus, you light our way to happiness. Help me to make room for you in my life this Advent.

We Seek Jesus During Advent

Advent is a time to seek Jesus and make room for him in our lives. During Advent we are reminded that Jesus will "light" our way to true happiness and peace.

How will I seek Jesus this Advent?

How can I make time for Jesus during my school day, at home, and on the weekends?

Jesus, My Light

Just like a star, Jesus is the light that shines in the darkness. How can I light the way for others as Jesus did?

Reading God's Word

Live as children of light. *Ephesians 5:8*

Mass During Advent

When you go to Mass during Advent, you may notice the brightness of the Advent candles. The lights symbolize Jesus and how he lights our way during the Advent season. You will also see the color purple, which is the color of Advent.

What We Experience

When you see the Advent candles in church, do you feel a sense of peace? Jesus is with you. Think about the light of Jesus as you color the festive candles purple or pink.

Ready for the Sacraments

During Advent we pay attention to how much we long to be close to God. In the Sacrament of Reconciliation, we can experience that closeness. We can be healed when we experience God's forgiving love with an open heart.

GO TO PAGE 244

Faith Summary

Advent is a time to seek Jesus and make room for him in our lives. Jesus is the light that shines in darkness to guide our way to true happiness and peace.

Ways of Being Like Jesus

Jesus is the light of the world. *Let his light shine through your kindness to others during this season.*

Prayer

Jesus, this Advent help me walk in your light. I want to seek you and make you the center of my life.

With My Family

Activity Suggest that your family make an Advent wreath. Take turns lighting the candles.

Ready for the Sacraments Write on slips of paper the names of people you are angry with and hold the papers tightly. Then try passing around a beanbag with closed fists. Talk about how it is just as difficult to receive forgiveness if your heart won't let go, open, and forgive.

Family Prayer Invite family members to grow during Advent. Each day pray together the prayer on this page.

The Church, Our Community in the Spirit

UNIT 3

Saint Ignatius of Loyola

Ignatius of Loyola is an important saint.

He learned about Jesus from his family.

Saint Ignatius of Loyola

Ignatius was born in Spain to a large Catholic family. He became a soldier, but he never forgot his Catholic upbringing.

Ignatius returned home after being wounded in battle. He read books about Jesus and the saints. Ignatius wanted to be like them. He decided to spend his life doing God's work.

Have you ever had an experience that changed your life, such as learning to ride a bike, welcoming a new sibling, or learning to read? How did you change?

We Worship God

Prayer

Jesus, my friend, help me stay close to you so that I will grow in faith.

The Holy Spirit Comes to Us

Jesus gave us the sacraments. They are special signs that God is with us. In the sacraments we receive the Holy Spirit, who brings us God's special gift of grace. This helps us be God's friends.

The Holy Spirit helps us act as God wants us to act. The good we find in our words or actions is called the **Fruits of the Holy Spirit.** We are able to be kind and loving because God is alive in us.

We are able to be kind and loving because God is alive in us.

The Sacrament of Baptism

Baptism is the first sacrament we celebrate. We become children of God and members of the Church when we are baptized. During the special way of celebrating, called a **rite,** a person is immersed in water or water is poured over the person's head. The grace we receive in the sacraments helps us stay close to God.

Baptism takes away **Original Sin.** This sin is in the world because Adam and Eve chose not to obey God.

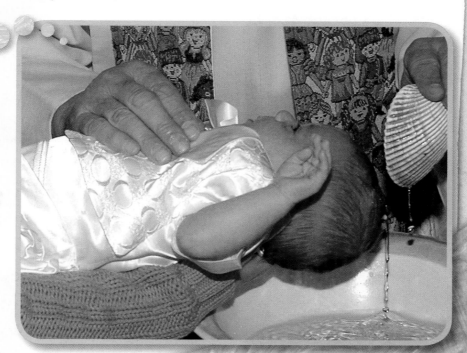

Ready for the Sacraments

At times we talk to friends and family heart-to-heart about our worries. The Sacrament of Reconciliation is a time when we can talk to God heart-to-heart.

GO TO PAGE 245

Jesus Is the Vine

Imagine you are in your favorite place. Then imagine Jesus is there with you. He wants to talk to you about the parable of the vine and the branches.

Jesus shows you a lovely vineyard. There are strong branches on the vine and clusters of ripe grapes. He shows you many healthy branches and how secure they are.

Jesus asks you to remember that he is the vine and you are one of the branches. He reminds you to stay close to him always. Invite him to look into your heart. You know you can tell Jesus whatever you want. Place your cares in his hands and listen for what he wants you to know. Enjoy being together.

Close to the Vine

Jesus wants us to stay close to him. How can your actions and words bring you closer to Jesus? What can you do to show Jesus that you love him?

Growing Close to Jesus

List things you can do to grow closer to Jesus each day.

1. _____

2. _____

3. _____

4. _____

5. _____

Living My Faith

Faith Summary

The grace we receive in the sacraments helps us stay close to God. Jesus told us the parable of the vine and the branches to help us stay close to him.

Words I Learned

Fruits of the Holy Spirit
Original Sin
rite

Ways of Being Like Jesus

Jesus' unending kindness brought others close to him. *Stay close to Jesus by being kind to others.*

Prayer

Thank you, God, for giving me Jesus. Keep me close as I learn more about you and Jesus, your Son.

With My Family

Activity To share household work, make a chore jar for your family. Have family members pick jobs to do from the jar.

Ready for the Sacraments At a family meal, have everyone finish this sentence for every other family member: "One thing I really appreciate about you is . . . ." Make sure you speak from the heart.

Family Prayer *Dear God, help us remember that Jesus is the vine and we are the branches. Help our family always stay close to Jesus.*

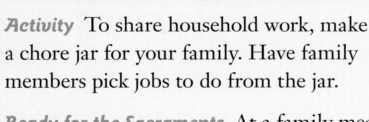

Chore Jar

Has a friend ever been unkind to you? Think of how it hurt your feelings. How did you become friends again?

Celebrating Reconciliation

Prayer

Jesus, my Savior, help me be aware of my sins. Teach me to ask for forgiveness when I am wrong.

Making Peace with God

We choose to turn away from God when we sin. We turn away from God when we commit a **mortal sin** or a **venial sin.**

Mortal sin is a very serious wrong. Venial sin is a less serious wrong. All sin hurts our relationship with God and with others.

Sin is forgiven when we celebrate the Sacrament of Reconciliation. In **confession** we tell God we are sorry. **Contrition** is the sadness we feel when we have sinned. In Reconciliation we make peace with God and with others. We promise God that we will try not to sin again.

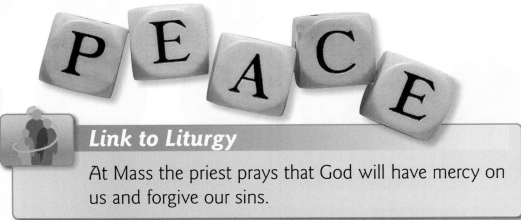

Link to Liturgy

At Mass the priest prays that God will have mercy on us and forgive our sins.

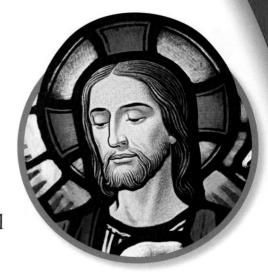

Before going to confession, it is important to make an **examination of conscience.**

Jesus is happy with us when we come to him in confession and tell him we are sorry for our sins. He will always forgive us.

Ready for the Sacraments

If Jason takes Chloe's soccer ball, it's not enough to say he is sorry. He must also give back the ball. After we confess our sins, the priest gives us a penance as a way to make up for our sins and change our lives. Then we can live in peace again.

GO TO PAGE 246

Saying "I'm Sorry"

God wants us to be sorry for our sins and to ask for his forgiveness. We pray a special prayer to tell him we are sorry for sinning. We ask God to help us do our best not to sin again.

Act of Contrition

My God,
I am sorry for my sins with all my heart.
In choosing to do wrong
and failing to do good,
I have sinned against you
whom I should love above all things.
I firmly intend, with your help,
to do penance,
to sin no more,
and to avoid whatever leads me to sin.
Our Savior Jesus Christ
suffered and died for us.
In his name, my God, have mercy.

Jesus Forgives

Jesus loves us and forgives us for our sins. After we are forgiven, he wants us to try to keep our hearts pure and to do our best not to sin again.

A Pure Heart

Write a letter to God. Ask him to help you keep a pure heart, free from sin. Tell him ways you will avoid sinning in the future.

Dear God,

_____

_____

_____

_____

_____

Love,

_____

Living My Faith

Faith Summary

When we celebrate the Sacrament of Reconciliation, God forgives our sins.

Words I Learned

confession   **contrition**   **examination of conscience**
mortal sin   **venial sin**

Ways of Being Like Jesus

Jesus forgave people who were sorry for their sins.
Be forgiving of others.

Prayer

Thank you, Jesus, for helping me forgive others as you forgive me.

With My Family

Activity Make cards that say *I'm sorry* and *I forgive you.* Have family members use the cards when they have a conflict.

Ready for the Sacraments Ask your family members to tell about a time they made something right for another person after doing something wrong. How did they feel afterward?

Family Prayer *Dear God, help us always love and forgive one another.*

Sometimes we do or say something to hurt our friends or family. How can we make it up to them?

The Sacrament of Reconciliation

Prayer

Jesus, my friend, teach me about forgiveness so that I may learn to make peace with God and with others.

We Are Forgiven

Jesus forgave the sins of others. He forgives our sins too. Jesus works through priests who forgive our sins in his name.

Our sins are forgiven as the priest extends his hands over us and prays the prayer of **absolution.** The prayer ends with the words:

"May God give you pardon and peace, and I absolve you from your sins in the name of the Father, and of the Son, and of the Holy Spirit."

Link to Liturgy

The priest must keep absolutely secret the sins that people have confessed to him. This is called the **seal of confession.**

After we confess our sins, the priest gives us a penance. This is a prayer we pray or a deed we do to make up for our sins. We tell God we want to live as his children.

The grace we receive in the Sacrament of Penance and Reconciliation will strengthen us when we are tempted to sin. It will help us avoid sin and grow closer to God.

We leave confession knowing we are at peace with God and with others.

Ready for the Sacraments

Have you ever carried a heavy package a long way? Was it difficult to carry? Did you feel relief when you put the package down? In the Sacrament of Reconciliation, we are relieved of the burden of our sins. We feel joy in the freedom of forgiveness.

GO TO PAGE 247

Making Peace with God

Contrition is the sadness we feel when we know we have sinned. We pray an Act of Contrition to tell God we are sorry.

God wants us to make peace with him. He wants us to make peace with others by asking forgiveness when we do something that is wrong.

Jesus knows what is in your heart. Know you are safe with him. Be still and spend some time with Jesus. Listen to what Jesus wants you to know.

Peace Be with You

How does being at peace with God and with others make you feel?

Making Peace

Use the words in the box to complete the sentences.

> contrition   peace   forgiveness

1. The sadness we feel when we know we have sinned is

   _____.

2. When we sin, we ask God and others for

   _____.

3. God wants us to make

   _____

   with him and with others.

Reading God's Word

The people are given knowledge that they are saved because their sins have been forgiven.

adapted from Luke 1:77

Living My Faith

Faith Summary

When we celebrate the Sacrament of Reconciliation, our sins are forgiven. We make peace with God and with others.

Words I Learned

absolution

seal of confession

Ways of Being Like Jesus

Jesus brought peace through forgiveness. *Be a peacemaker with your family and friends.*

Prayer

Thank you, God, my Father, for forgiving me. Help me to be a more peaceful child of yours.

With My Family

Activity This week forgive a family member or ask someone to forgive you.

Ready for the Sacraments Ask your family members about a time they felt contrition, asked forgiveness, and made peace with another person. Talk about what it felt like to apologize and to be forgiven.

Family Prayer *Dear God, help us remember that you love us and will always forgive our sins.*

What have you needed help with recently? Who usually helps you?

Mary Shows Us the Way

Prayer

God, my Heavenly Father, teach me about Mary so that I may learn to follow her example.

Mary Visits Elizabeth

The angel Gabriel told Mary that she was going to be the mother of Jesus. Soon after that, Mary went to visit her cousin Elizabeth.

Elizabeth was very happy to see Mary. She praised Mary for her love of God. She called her blessed.

Mary said to Elizabeth, "God is great. He is my Savior. All people will call me blessed. God has done great things for me."

Then Mary said, "God's name is holy. His mercy will last forever."

adapted from Luke 1:39–55

Did You Know?

Catholics around the world honor Mary.

Magnificat

The words Mary used to praise God have become a special prayer. Catholics call this prayer the **Magnificat**.

In the prayer, we pray:

My soul proclaims the greatness of the Lord, and my spirit rejoices in God my Savior. The Lord has shown mercy and strength and done good things for all people.

adapted from the Magnificat

Ready for the Sacraments

Jesus' mother, Mary, teaches us that sometimes it is good to think quietly in our hearts. One way to stay close to God is to remember the good things God does for you. Make time each day to be quiet. Be aware that God loves you.

GO TO PAGE 248

Mother Mary

Mary had the courage and love to do what God asked her to do. In your imagination go to Mary and talk with her about saying yes to God. Ask her what it was like for her to do this.

Tell her it is not always easy for you to say yes to God. Stay with Mary for a while. Pray together to God to help you say yes too.

Praise God

We can follow Mary's example by praising God as she did.

Poem of Praise

Use the words in the box to complete this poem of praise.

> Jesus name way

Mary praised God,
And we do the same,
For he is our Savior,

And holy is his _____.

Through actions and words,

Mary shows us the _____
To share God's great love,
With one another each day.

If we obey God,
As Mary shows us,
We stay with the Father

And his Son, _____.

Living My Faith

Faith Summary

Elizabeth called Mary blessed. We honor Mary in a special prayer called the Magnificat.

Word I Learned

Magnificat

Ways of Being Like Jesus

Jesus loved his mother very much. *Honor and love Mary, the Mother of the Church.*

Prayer

Thank you, God, for the example of Mary. Help me say yes to you.

With My Family

Activity Talk with family members about ways to honor Mary in your home.

Ready for the Sacraments Explore how Mary is honored in the country or countries your ancestors are from. Find an image of Mary to display in a place of honor in your home.

Family Prayer Dear God, help our family love and praise you as Mary did.

Celebrating Christmas

Christmas is celebrated on December 25. The season of Christmas begins on December 24 and lasts through the Feast of the Baptism of the Lord, which is celebrated the Sunday after the Epiphany.

Prayer

Dear Jesus, help me remember at Christmas that you are the best gift I can receive.

We Celebrate During Christmas

How does your family celebrate the joy of Christmas? Does your family read the Nativity story? Do friends or relatives come to visit? Do you eat a special meal with your family?

We gather as families to celebrate Jesus in our midst.

Draw a picture of your family celebrating the joy of Christmas.

Reading God's Word

They will name him Emmanuel, which means "God is with us."

adapted from Matthew 1:23

Mass During Christmas

As families gather to celebrate Mass, a sense of joy and excitement fills the church. We have prepared for Jesus during Advent, and now we celebrate his coming.

What We Experience

When you look around your church, you may see a **Nativity scene.** Do you see Mary, Joseph, and the baby Jesus? Are the shepherds there, taking care of their sheep? What else do you see in this well-known scene?

Color the Nativity scene.

Ready for the Sacraments

We must prepare to receive God's most precious gift—his Son, Jesus, in the Eucharist. We begin by praying "Jesus, come into my heart. Help me welcome you every day of my life."

GO TO PAGE 249

Faith Summary

Christmas is a time to gather as families to celebrate the birth of Jesus.

Words I Learned

Nativity scene

Ways of Being Like Jesus

Jesus brought joy to the world. *Share your joy with others.*

Prayer

Dear God, thank you for giving us your Son, Jesus. Help me to share my light with others.

With My Family

Activity When you go to Mass during Christmas, look around your church. After Mass talk about what you saw and felt.

Ready for the Sacraments Prepare a manger for the infant Jesus, keeping the crib empty until Christmas. For each kind act performed during Advent, place a handful of straw or a piece of felt in the crib to prepare a welcoming place for the Christ child.

Family Prayer *Dear God, thank you for giving us the greatest gift of all—your Son, Jesus.*

Sacraments, Our Way of Life

Pope Saint Pius X

Pope Saint Pius X was an important pope. He helped the Church bring people closer to God. He was named a saint in 1954.

Pope Saint Pius X

Pius X wanted Catholics to receive Holy Communion often. He believed that children should be able to receive Holy Communion around age seven. He wanted them to be close to Jesus.

Pope Pius X spread God's love to the world. He spent his life helping others. He started charities to care for people who were poor.

Have you ever been a member of a group? Are you part of a choir or a sports team? What are the good things about being a member of a group?

New Life in Jesus

Prayer

Jesus, my friend, help me learn about the sacraments so that I may appreciate what you are giving me.

Special Signs from God

A sacrament is a special sign. It shows that God is with us. Jesus gave the sacraments to the Church.

The **Sacraments of Initiation** are Baptism, **Confirmation**, and the Eucharist. These sacraments bring us into God's family. They give us grace. Grace is a gift we receive from God.

Baptism

Baptism is the beginning of our new life with Jesus. We are saved from our sins in Baptism. Baptism gives us sanctifying grace. This is the gift of God's new life in us.

We become a member of the Church when we are baptized. We become part of God's family.

Reading God's Word

The Spirit says, "Come." Whoever is thirsty may come forward and receive life-giving water.

adapted from Revelation 22:17

Confirmation

Confirmation makes us stronger in faith through God's sanctifying grace. Confirmation helps us become better Christians.

Eucharist

We receive the **Body and Blood of Christ** in the Eucharist. This is called **Holy Communion**.

The bread and wine of the Eucharist become the Body and Blood of Jesus Christ. This happens through the words of consecration prayed by the priest.

Ready for the Sacraments

Jesus promises to be with us always, and he is close to us in a special way in the sacraments. Quiet your mind and open your heart. Say, "Jesus, I look forward to receiving you in my First Holy Communion. Help me to be prepared to receive you."

GO TO PAGE 250

God Gave Us Water

God gave us water to drink because we need it to live.

Think about the many things you can do with water. Maybe you like to swim in it or make water balloons. You can take a long, cool drink of water on a hot day. What other things do you do with water?

Now think about the water that was poured over you when you were baptized. You were given new life with Jesus. You became part of God's family. In your imagination meet Jesus in your favorite place. Tell him how happy you are to be God's child. Listen with your heart to what he tells you.

The Sacraments in Our Lives

The sacraments are special signs. Through these signs God gives us grace. Each sacrament builds our faith.

Making Peace

Draw a line from each word to each correct answer. The first one is done for you.

Holy Communion ● ● The beginning of our new life with Jesus

Confirmation ● ● Sacrament in which bread and wine become the Body and Blood of Jesus Christ

Sacraments of Initiation ● ● Makes us stronger in faith

Eucharist ● ● Baptism, Confirmation, and the Eucharist

Baptism ● ● The Body and Blood of Jesus Christ, which we receive in the Eucharist

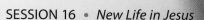

Faith Summary

Baptism, Confirmation, and the Eucharist are the Sacraments of Initiation.

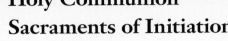

Words I Learned

Body and Blood of Christ
Confirmation

Holy Communion
Sacraments of Initiation

Ways of Being Like Jesus

Jesus gave us the sacraments to remind us that God is always with us. *Talk with Jesus in your heart throughout the day.*

Prayer

Thank you, God, for your gift of grace. Help me always stay close to you.

With My Family

Activity As a family, volunteer your time to help with a parish ministry.

Ready for the Sacraments Ask each family member to describe a time he or she was really happy to be together as a family. Thank Jesus for being present in the life of your family and in each of the situations described.

Family Prayer *Dear God, help us remember we are always part of your family.*

Imagine a new child has moved into your neighborhood. How can you welcome your new neighbor? What can you do to make him or her feel at home?

Jesus Loves the Church

Prayer

Jesus, my guide, help me welcome you into my heart and my life.

Inviting Jesus to Dinner

After Jesus died, two of his **disciples** were walking along a road. They met a man. The disciples did not know who he was. The disciples told him about all that had happened to Jesus. They invited the man to join them for dinner.

The man sat down with the disciples at the dinner table. He broke bread, blessed it, and gave it to them. When he did this, they knew he was Jesus. They knew Jesus had risen.

adapted from Luke 24:13–31

Reading God's Word

Jesus' followers came together to learn, to pray, and to break bread. *adapted from Acts of the Apostles 2:42*

Jesus Is with Us

The Holy Spirit comes to us in Baptism. Every day the grace of the Holy Spirit helps us love others. When we love others, we welcome Jesus into our lives.

The most important way we remember that Jesus is with us is in the celebration of the Eucharist, or the **Sacrifice of the Mass**. It is celebrated every day. The Mass helps us remember Jesus died for us and saved us from our sins.

As Catholics, we should participate in the Mass and receive Holy Communion every Sunday.

Ready for the Sacraments

In the Gospel stories, we hear the messages Jesus wants to tell us. He wants us to be kind and not judge others. He wants us to love everyone—even our enemies. He wants us to know that God is a loving father who wants the best for us.

GO TO PAGE 251

Bless Us, O Lord

Mealtime is a good time to share. You can help set the table or help make the meal. You can also share thoughts with your family during meals.

Praying is another important part of gathering for meals. Before eating, take time to thank God for the food you have. With your family pray this prayer before meals.

Prayer Before Meals

Bless us, O Lord,
and these your gifts
which we are about to receive
from your goodness.
Through Christ our Lord.
Amen.

Welcome, Jesus!

Like the disciples, you can invite Jesus into your life too.

A Message for Jesus

Imagine Jesus is coming to visit your home. Write a welcome message for Jesus on the entrance to your house. Color and decorate the house for your friend, Jesus.

Faith Summary

The Holy Spirit comes to us in Baptism. His grace helps us love Jesus and others. At Mass we remember that Jesus died to save us from our sins.

Words I Learned

disciple
ministry*
Sacrifice of the Mass

Ways of Being Like Jesus

Jesus welcomed new people into his life. *Talk with a child at school whom you don't know well.*

Prayer

Loving Jesus, you are always welcome in my life. Help me welcome others.

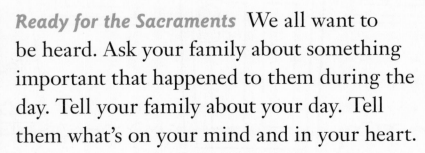

With My Family

Activity As a family, take a treat to a new neighbor.

Ready for the Sacraments We all want to be heard. Ask your family about something important that happened to them during the day. Tell your family about your day. Tell them what's on your mind and in your heart.

Family Prayer *Dear Jesus, may the grace you send strengthen our love toward you and others.*

* This word is taught with the Art Print. See page 251.

Have you ever hosted a party or a sleepover? What did you have to do to get ready for your guests? Was it exciting to prepare for this fun time?

Gathering for Mass

Prayer

God, my Father, help me discover the many ways I can praise you and ask for your blessings at Mass.

The Mass Begins

As Catholics we go to Mass every Sunday and on special days. Volunteers, such as altar servers, readers, and song leaders, are assigned to help the priest. They come to the altar with the priest during the Entrance Chant.

First, the priest greets everyone. Then he leads a prayer for the forgiveness of our sins. Next, we pray the *Gloria*. This prayer gives glory to God the Father; Jesus, his Son; and the Holy Spirit.

Hearing God's Message

A reader walks to the **ambo**, a place where he or she will read. The stories come from a special book. It is called the *Lectionary for Mass.*

When the reader finishes, the priest walks to the ambo to read a story about Jesus' life and message. Then he explains how all the readings have an important message about how we live every day. This talk is called the **homily.**

Reading God's Word

You have known about God's messages since you were a child. These messages help you realize what is important.

adapted from 2 Timothy 3:14–17

God's Message

Responding to God's Word

After the homily we express our belief in the teachings of the Church. We do this by saying, "I believe."

The Bible readings and the Homily are two parts of the **Liturgy of the Word**. This is the time during the Mass when we listen to God's Word from the Bible. The Liturgy of the Word ends when we pray together for anyone in need of prayers.

I believe

 Ready for the Sacraments

Sunday is the special day of the week we make time to care for our relationship with God. We enjoy the gift of time and rest that God wants to give us. We say thank you to God by gathering at Mass to worship him and listen to his Word.

GO TO PAGE 252

Living God's Message

At Mass we gather to praise God. We also receive messages from him. Mass brings us closer to God. It helps us do what God wants.

We can praise God in our everyday lives too. Think about something you want to tell God. Maybe you want to praise him for a good thing that has happened to you.

Think about how you can live God's message every day. What can you do to bring God's message into your life?

Now spend some quiet time with God. Ask him to help you understand his special message for you. Listen for what God wants you to know. Then just be still with him for a while.

The Mass

What happens during Mass?

Put the steps in order. Number them 1 to 7.

_____ The priest reads a story about Jesus' life and message.

_____ We say "I believe" to the teachings of the Church.

_____ The priest explains the readings in the homily.

_____ We pray the *Gloria,* a prayer praising God.

_____ We pray to God to help those in need.

_____ We sing as the priest comes to the altar.

_____ A reader reads stories from the Bible.

Link to Liturgy

We are asked to respond to each reading during the Liturgy of the Word. When the reader says, "The Word of the Lord," we say, "Thanks be to God."

Faith Summary

At Mass we praise God and ask for his blessing. The readings make Jesus present to us in a special way.

Words I Learned	**Ways of Being Like Jesus**
ambo	Jesus worshiped God in the Temple. *Attend weekly Mass and spend time with God.*
Evangelists*	
homily	
Lectionary for Mass	
Liturgy of the Word	

Prayer

Thank you, Jesus, for giving us your message. Help me listen carefully. I want to follow you.

With My Family

Activity As a family, greet the priest after Mass.

Ready for the Sacraments On Sunday we set aside the activities of the week and spend time with our family worshiping God together. Talk to your family about making Sunday a day to think about God and his creation.

Family Prayer *God, we thank you for the gift of Mass. Help us listen with our hearts and minds.*

* This word is taught with the Art Print. See page 252.

Have you ever given something to a friend? Have you shared something special with a family member? How did giving and sharing bring you closer to that person?

Celebrating the Eucharist

Prayer

Jesus, my Savior, help me share your love with others.

Liturgy of the Eucharist

Suki and her family go to Mass together every Sunday. Last week, as the **Liturgy of the Eucharist** began, they brought the gifts of bread and wine to the priest at the **altar**. Suki and her family listened as the priest asked God to accept and bless the gifts.

During the consecration the priest repeated the words of Jesus at the Last Supper. The bread and wine became the Body and Blood of Christ. This is called **transubstantiation**. The priest invited everyone to pray the Lord's Prayer and to share a sign of peace. Soon it was time to receive Holy Communion. They received the Body and Blood of Christ.

After praying silently, the priest gave everyone a blessing. He told them to go in peace and glorify the Lord by their lives.

transubstantiation

Did You Know?

Sunday is special because it is the Lord's Day.

Attending Mass

The Church calls us to attend Mass on Sundays and **Holy Days of Obligation**. These are days when we go to Mass to remember great things God has done for us.

Can you name a Holy Day of Obligation?

Obligation

Ready for the Sacraments

At the Last Supper Jesus had with his friends, he washed the feet of the apostles. He wanted to show them how to love and to serve one another. One way to prepare to receive Jesus in the Eucharist is to love and to serve others as he did.

GO TO PAGE 253

Preparing to Receive Jesus

Before receiving Holy Communion, the priest says,

Behold the Lamb of God,
behold him who takes away the
*   sins of the world.*
Blessed are those called to the
*   supper of the Lamb.*

We respond by praying,

Lord, I am not worthy
that you should enter under my roof,
but only say the word
and my soul shall be healed.

Think about these words. How special is Jesus' gift of the Eucharist? How can you thank Jesus for giving himself to you?

Now spend some time with Jesus. Imagine you are talking with him. Talk to him about what you are feeling. Listen to what Jesus wants you to know.

The Eucharist

During the Eucharistic Prayer, the bread and wine become the Body and Blood of Jesus Christ.

Jesus' Gift

Color the picture below. Write a short prayer thanking Jesus for giving himself to you.

_____

_____

_____

_____

_____

Living My Faith

Faith Summary

The Mass is the most important way Catholics pray.

Words I Learned

altar
Holy Days of Obligation
Liturgy of the Eucharist
transubstantiation

Ways of Being Like Jesus

Jesus gave himself to us. *Give of yourself to help others.*

Prayer

Thank you, Jesus, for giving yourself to me. Place in my heart a great love for the Eucharist.

With My Family

Activity Give up one hour of your free time this week to help someone in your family.

Ready for the Sacraments Follow Jesus' example of service. As a family, shine each other's shoes. You can do this together or as a surprise to the other person. Let this act of service be a way you prepare for Mass.

Family Prayer *Dear God, thank you for sending Jesus to us.*

Celebrating Lent and Holy Week

During Lent we prepare to celebrate the Resurrection of Jesus at Easter. The season of Lent lasts 40 days beginning with Ash Wednesday. The last week of Lent is Holy Week. During this week we celebrate Holy Thursday, Good Friday, and the Easter Vigil.

Prayer

Dear Jesus, I want to grow closer to you during Lent. Help me be the person you want me to be.

We Grow in Goodness During Lent and Holy Week

Lent is a time to ask for God's help in becoming the person he calls us to be. To prepare for this special time, ask yourself these questions.

How can I be a better friend to others?

How can I show more respect to my family?

A Time to Change

Lent reminds us that following Jesus means changing our lives. How will you change this Lent?

_____

_____

_____

_____

_____

_____

_____

Reading God's Word

Put away your old self and be renewed in Christ.

adapted from Ephesians 4:22–24

Mass During Lent and Holy Week

During Lent and Holy Week, pay special attention to the beginning of Mass. At this time we admit our sinfulness and ask for God's mercy. We pray for God's help to be more faithful in living as Jesus taught us.

What We Experience

During Lent your church looks very plain. Often we do not see flowers or decorations in the sanctuary. The priest wears purple vestments during Lent.

Important Days

Unscramble the words below to write five important days in the season of Lent.

sAh nyddWesea _____

mPal ydaSnu _____

yHol ydushTar _____

doGo dyairF _____

sarEte lViig _____

Ready for the Sacraments

Jesus always did his Father's will, even when it was hard. At Mass we learn to be faithful to God our Father, just like Jesus. We celebrate how Jesus' dying and rising gave us freedom from sin and the promise of eternal life.

GO TO PAGE 254

Faith Summary

Lent is a time to ask God's help to become the person he calls you to be. During Lent we change our lives to follow Jesus more closely.

Ways of Being Like Jesus

Jesus called people to change their lives. *Play with a classmate you do not usually spend time with.*

Prayer

Dear Jesus, thank you for this season of change. Help me grow in goodness toward others.

With My Family

Activity When you go to Mass during Lent and Holy Week, look around your church. Talk about what you see.

Ready for the Sacraments As a family, think of ways you each sacrifice for one another. Give your time and help to one another. You can join your sacrifice to that of Jesus, who sacrificed his life for us.

Family Prayer Invite family members to grow by taking turns leading the mealtime prayer.

Morality, Our Lived Faith

Saint Martin of Tours

Saint Martin of Tours cared for others. Martin's kind acts helped him find out what God wanted him to do.

Saint Martin of Tours

Martin lived a long time ago. He became a soldier at a young age.

One cold night Martin met a man who was freezing. Martin cut his coat and gave half of it to the man. That same night Martin saw Jesus in a dream. Jesus was wearing half of Martin's coat.

Martin became a Christian after his dream. Later he was made a bishop in France. As bishop he helped many people. Saint Martin became one of the most important Church leaders of his time. We celebrate his feast day on November 11.

Have you ever helped someone who was sad or hurt? How did you help this person? How did it make you feel about yourself?

Being Like Jesus

Prayer

Jesus, model of love, help me learn about the things you said and did so that I can become more like you.

The Good Samaritan

A man asked Jesus, "What must I do to live with God forever?"

Jesus answered, "What does the law say?"

The man said, "You should love the Lord with all your strength. You should love your neighbor as much as you love yourself."

Jesus told the man that he had given the right answer. Jesus told him he would go to Heaven if he did these things.

Then the man asked Jesus, "Who is my neighbor?"

Jesus answered by telling this story. "A Jewish man was traveling on a road. He was attacked by robbers. They left him hurt in the road. A Temple official walked by and ignored the hurt man. Another man passed by and did not help him."

"Then a good man from Samaria saw him. He wanted to help. So the Good Samaritan bandaged the man's wounds, lifted him onto his donkey, and took him to an inn."

Then Jesus asked, "Which of these three men acted like a good neighbor?"

"The one who showed mercy," said the man who was questioning Jesus.

"Yes," said Jesus. "Go and be like this man."

adapted from Luke 10:25–37

Good Samaritan

Ready for the Sacraments

Jesus is the example of what it means to be human. He is loving, kind, and holy. The more we get to know Jesus, the more we can be like him. Receiving the Eucharist with an open and a loving heart is an important way we grow to be more like Jesus.

GO TO PAGE 255

Being a Good Samaritan

Jesus asks us to show mercy in what we do and say. He wants us to act as the Good Samaritan did.

In your imagination meet Jesus in a place where you like to be. Tell Jesus you know he wants you to be kind and good to others.

Tell him about something nice you did for someone. Then tell Jesus when it is hard for you to be nice. Ask him to help you. Listen to what Jesus says to you.

Acting as Jesus Would

Saint Martin of Tours reached out to a suffering stranger. The Good Samaritan acted with love and mercy. Both of these people acted as Jesus would.

Making a Difference

Mark the box that shows an example of someone acting as Jesus would.

Faith Summary

Jesus shows us how to love others through his words and actions. He wants us to help our neighbors. He wants us to care for people whom others may have forgotten.

Word I Learned

Beatitudes*

Ways of Being Like Jesus

Jesus taught us to show mercy to others. *Be a Good Samaritan every day.*

Prayer

Thank you, Jesus, for your parables. Help me be a Good Samaritan to others.

With My Family

Activity As a family, give comfort and assistance to a person or family in need.

Ready for the Sacraments Make a list of traits that describe Jesus, such as loving, faithful, and merciful. Remember those traits the next time you receive the Eucharist because in this sacrament we become like Jesus.

Family Prayer *Dear God, help us show Jesus' love to everyone we meet.*

* This word is taught with the Art Print. See page 255.

Think of a good choice you have made. What helped you make the right choice?

We Share God's Life

Prayer

Dear Jesus, help me stay close to you and make good choices in all I do and say.

129

Guided by God's Gifts

God has given us the Church and the Bible. These gifts teach us the difference between right and wrong. They help us make a **moral choice.**

The important people in our lives can help us when we make choices. These people include family members, teachers, catechists, and priests. Praying to the Holy Spirit also guides us in making good choices.

Steps for Making Good Choices

Ask the Holy Spirit to help you make a good choice. Then ask yourself these questions before making an important decision:

1. Is the thing I am choosing to do a good thing?
2. Am I choosing to do it for the right reasons?
3. Am I choosing to do it at the right time and in the right place?

Your **conscience** is your inner sense of right and wrong. Listen to your conscience. Let it guide you to do what is best.

Ready for the Sacraments

The Sacrament of the Eucharist joins us all together as one. All the people in the Church may not know one another, but they are all part of the same body— the Body of Christ. That means we are meant to love and to help one another as Jesus would.

GO TO PAGE 256

Good Choices

The Holy Spirit helps us make good choices. It is not always easy to do the right thing. By calling on the Holy Spirit, we can learn to act as God wants us to.

Think of a difficult choice you had to make. Did you ask anyone for help?

Now think about your choice. Was it the right thing to do? Was it what God wanted you to do?

Take a few moments to speak to the Holy Spirit. Tell him how you feel about your decision.

Now ask the Holy Spirit to guide you the next time you must make a difficult choice. Ask him to help you make the right decision.

Choosing Like Jesus

When you are faced with making a difficult choice, think about what Jesus would do.

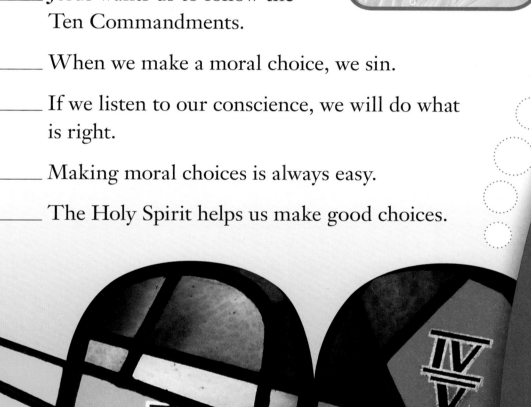

Moral Choices

Write **T** if the sentence is true.

Write **F** if the sentence is false.

1. _____ Jesus wants us to follow the Ten Commandments.

2. _____ When we make a moral choice, we sin.

3. _____ If we listen to our conscience, we will do what is right.

4. _____ Making moral choices is always easy.

5. _____ The Holy Spirit helps us make good choices.

Living My Faith

Faith Summary

The Church and the Bible teach us the difference between right and wrong. Praying to the Holy Spirit helps us make the right choices.

Words I Learned

conscience
moral choice

Ways of Being Like Jesus

Jesus always prayed for guidance. *Ask the Holy Spirit to help you make a good choice today.*

Prayer

Thank you, God, for all of the ways you help me.

With My Family

Activity Think of an organization of people who have made a choice to help others. Help this organization in whatever way you can.

Ready for the Sacraments Before a family meal, ask everyone to hold hands. Ask your family to imagine the love you have for one another flowing around the circle. Say a prayer that you will always remain connected to God and to one another.

Family Prayer *Dear God, help us make good, moral choices.*

Think of a time when someone was kind to you. What did you think of this person? How did this person's actions make you want to treat others?

Following Jesus

Prayer

Jesus, help me treat others with love and kindness as you do.

The Great Commandment

The **Old Testament** is the story of God's love for the Jewish people. The **New Testament** is the story of Jesus' life. It also tells how the early Church lived like Jesus.

In the Old Testament, God gave Moses the Ten Commandments. In the New Testament, Jesus gave us the **Great Commandment.** It teaches us how to follow God and to care for others. Thinking about the Great Commandment helps us make moral choices. We make the right choice when we love God and others.

Reading God's Word

Love God with all your heart, soul, and mind. Love your neighbor as yourself. This is the greatest commandment.

adapted from Matthew 22:37–38

The Beatitudes

Jesus wants us to be happy, so he taught us the Beatitudes.

Jesus said, "Blessed are those who are kind to others. They will be rewarded."

"Blessed are those who do the right thing even when it is difficult. They will be with God one day."

"Blessed are those who are fair to others. They will be treated fairly."

"Blessed are those who work for peace. They are God's children."

adapted from Matthew 5:1–10

When Jesus gave us the Beatitudes, he taught us how to be happy by treating one another with love and kindness.

Ready for the Sacraments

When someone treats us with love, it helps us be more loving to others. Receiving the love of Jesus in the Eucharist helps us be more loving to others. We share that love with those we meet at home, at school, and at play.

GO TO PAGE 257

Making a Choice

Imagine you are sitting on a bench in the middle of a city. You are thinking about a choice you must make.

Jesus and his disciples cross the street and sit near you. Jesus is speaking with his disciples about how to live a happy life.

Jesus invites you to join in their conversation. Perhaps you ask him about the choice you need to make. You stay with Jesus quietly, listening to his words. He has the answers to your questions. Be at peace with Jesus. Listen to what he wants you to know.

Live in Peace

The Beatitudes teach us how to live in peace with others.

Doing What Jesus Teaches

In the stories below, Nadia, Arturo, and Jerome each have to make a difficult choice. Write the choice each of them can make to follow the Beatitudes.

1. Will forgets to bring his crayons to art class. Nadia just got new crayons, and she does not want anyone to ruin them.

   _____

   _____

2. Arturo's little sister needs help with her homework. He really wants to go outside to play.

   _____

   _____

3. Two children get into a fight on the playground. Jerome and some other children stop and watch.

   _____

   _____

Meet a Saint

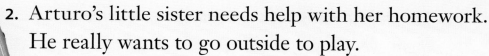

Saint Elizabeth Ann Seton always found time to help others. She started the first Catholic grade school in the United States. Elizabeth Ann Seton was the first American-born person to be named a saint.

Living My Faith

Faith Summary

In the Great Commandment, Jesus told us to love God and others. Jesus gave us the Beatitudes to help us live a happy life.

Words I Learned

Great Commandment
New Testament
Old Testament

Ways of Being Like Jesus

Jesus worked for peace. *Make peace today with someone you hurt.*

Prayer

Thank you, Jesus, for the Beatitudes. Help me to live them every day.

With My Family

Activity Keep track of the choices you make this week. What helps you decide how to act?

Ready for the Sacraments When you gather for a family meal, ask "Whom did you help today?" This question will remind us that we live not only for ourselves, but that we are meant to bring God's love to the world.

Family Prayer Dear God, *help us show your love to one another this week.*

Think of a time when someone played with your toys. Did this person respect you and your belongings? How can you respect others?

Making Choices

Prayer

Jesus, you want all people to live in peace. Teach me to be respectful of others.

A Community of Believers

Peter wanted to teach Christians about God's plan for them. So he wrote a letter.

Peter wrote, "Whoever loves their life should not tell lies or say evil things. Do what is right and stay away from evil. Bring peace into the world."

adapted from 1 Peter 3:10–11

Reading God's Word

If you want to be happy, do not say bad things or tell lies. Always be peaceful with one another, and do not sin.

adapted from Psalm 34:12–15

Living in Kindness

God wants us to be **peacemakers** and to live in kindness. He wants us to be kind to one another and to enjoy the kindness others show us.

When we steal, lie, or say unkind things, we sin. God wants us to make up for what we have done. We ask for forgiveness. We return what was stolen. We stop saying hurtful things. Then we can live in kindness as God wants us to.

Kindness

Ready for the Sacraments

As we become more like Jesus, we follow him more closely. We make choices based on what we know Jesus wants for the world. He wants us to help others and to stay close to God the Father in prayer.

GO TO PAGE 258

Quiet Time with Jesus

Imagine you are sitting quietly by yourself. As you sit there, Jesus walks up to you.

You begin talking to Jesus about how you have grown closer to him this year. Maybe you talk about the happy and sad times you have had. Know that you can share whatever you want with Jesus.

You can ask him for whatever you need.

Spend some quiet time listening to Jesus. Talk to him from your heart. Listen to what he wants you to know.

Respecting Others

How can you show respect to others at home, in school, and in your community?

Showing Respect

Write **R** if the person is being respectful.

Write **NR** if the person is not being respectful.

1. _____ Tucker makes fun of Corey's haircut.

2. _____ Sara reads her sister's journal when she is not home.

3. _____ Kevin thanks Holly for helping him.

4. _____ Yoon-Soo eats his brother's sandwich without asking him.

5. _____ Maria cleans her sister's bike after borrowing it.

Link to Liturgy

The **sign of peace** at Mass is one way we show respect for others.

Faith Summary

Jesus teaches us to respect people and to make peace. We will be happy if we show kindness in our words and actions.

Words I Learned

peacemaker
sign of peace

Ways of Being Like Jesus

Jesus respected everyone. *Show respect in your words and deeds.*

Prayer

Thank you, Jesus, for all you have taught me. Help me to respect everyone I meet.

With My Family

Activity Discuss with your family how you can show respect for one another and what you can do to live peacefully together.

Ready for the Sacraments Sometimes we are tempted to be better or more popular than others. Jesus offers another vision of life, one that helps us recognize others' gifts, and celebrates who we are and who we belong to—God our loving father.

Family Prayer Dear God, help us use respectful words and actions in our home.

Celebrating Easter

Easter is the most important day of the Church year. It is celebrated on the first Sunday after the first full moon of spring. The Easter season begins with the celebration of the Easter Vigil on Holy Saturday and continues for the next 50 days, ending on Pentecost Sunday.

Prayer

Risen Jesus, you are alive and with us. Help me be glad and rejoice.

We Reflect During Easter

Easter is a time to reflect on the gift of **eternal life.** Jesus died on the cross for our sins. He rose from the dead and returned to Heaven to hold a place for all of us.

What will Heaven be like?

Why is it so special?

Eternal Life in Heaven

Imagine Heaven. Draw a picture about what you see, hear, and feel.

Reading God's Word

I give them eternal life, so they will always live, even if they die.   *adapted from John 10:28*

Mass During Easter

At Mass during Easter, you may hear joyful music. The parish rejoices that Jesus is risen. How does Easter Sunday Mass at your church feel different from other Sunday celebrations?

What We Experience

When you look around your church, you may see beautiful Easter flowers. You may also see a cross draped with a white cloth. This reminds us that Jesus is risen.

Color your own Resurrection symbol below.

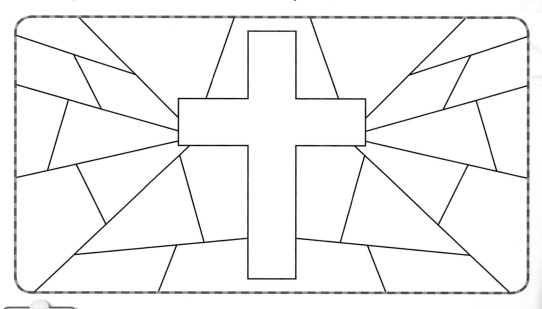

Ready for the Sacraments

The sacraments are ways that Jesus comes close to us. In Baptism we become members of God's family. In the Sacrament of Reconciliation, Jesus forgives our sins and heals our hearts. In the Eucharist, Jesus chooses to live within us, strengthening us to bring his love to the world.

GO TO PAGE 259

Faith Summary

Easter is a time of great joy. We remember that Jesus is risen. It is also a time to reflect on the gift of eternal life.

Words I Learned

eternal life

Ways of Being Like Jesus

Jesus' new life fills us with joy.
Spread joy to those you meet today.

Prayer

Dear Jesus, thank you for the gift of eternal life. Help me live with faith and hope.

With My Family

Activity When you go to Mass during Easter, look around your church. Find examples of the details described on page 149. Talk about what you see and hear.

Ready for the Sacraments Discuss what your family meals together mean to you. Tell your family that the time you spend together around the table can help you prepare to celebrate and live out the sacraments—gifts from God that bring abundant life.

Family Prayer Invite family members to pray the Rosary together during Easter.

The Year in Our Church

Liturgical Calendar

The liturgical calendar shows us the feasts and seasons of the Church year.

Ordinary Time

Lent

Ash Wednesday

Holy Week

Palm Sunday
Holy Thursday
Good Friday
Holy Saturday

Christmas

Epiphany

Christmas

Easter Sunday

Easter

Advent

Winter

Spring

Fall

Summer

First Sunday of Advent

Ascension
Pentecost

All Souls Day
All Saints Day

Ordinary Time

Liturgical Year

We get our hearts ready to welcome Jesus during **Advent.**

Christmas celebrates Jesus' birth. The Epiphany celebrates Jesus' coming for all people of the world.

Lent prepares us for Easter. It is a time to do extra good deeds.

During **Holy Week** we remember the suffering and Death of Jesus.

On **Easter** we recall with joy Jesus' rising from the dead.

Pentecost is the feast of the Holy Spirit's coming to guide the Church.

All Saints Day celebrates all the holy people who died and now live with God in Heaven.

Ordinary Time is time set aside for everyday living as followers of Jesus.

Advent

We get ready to celebrate Jesus' birth in Advent. A long time ago, Saint John the Baptist helped people get ready for Jesus.

Prayer

Dear God, help me this Advent to pray and to share.

Preparing for Jesus' Birth

Sometimes it is hard to wait. When we have a birthday party, we get ready. Then we wait and wait. We are excited. We celebrate when our birthday guests arrive.

During Advent we get ready to celebrate the birth of Jesus. Advent is our time of waiting.

Waiting for Jesus

People asked John the Baptist how to get ready for Jesus. John told the people to share and to help one another. He told them to be honest. He told them not to steal from one another.

adapted from Luke 3:10–14

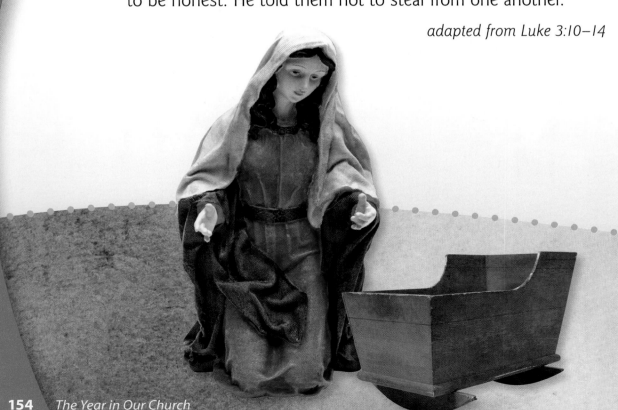

The Advent Wreath

The Advent wreath has four candles—three purple and one pink. There is one candle for each of the four weeks of Advent. During Advent we prepare to celebrate Jesus' birth. We pray and do good deeds for others. This is what John the Baptist told the people to do.

Welcoming Jesus

Draw a picture that shows how you prepare at home for Jesus' birth.

Prayer Service

Leader: *John the Baptist helped people change their lives. He helped them get ready for Jesus. Let us pray this Advent that we will be ready to follow Jesus.*

Reader: *A reading from the Book of Psalms.*

I wait for you, O Lord. Teach me to follow your path. Guide me in your truth because you are God, my Savior. I will wait for you all day.

adapted from Psalm 25:4–5

All: *Jesus is the light of the world. The world is brighter when we are a light for others.*

Christmas

The three Wise Men traveled far to find Jesus. They wanted to honor him.

Prayer

Jesus, my Savior, help me be a gift to others as you are to me.

The Three Wise Men

The Wise Men were looking for the new king. They wanted to worship him. They saw his star.

The star led the Wise Men to Bethlehem. There they saw Jesus with Mary and Joseph. They gave Jesus gifts of gold, frankincense, and myrrh.

The Wise Men then returned home.

adapted from Matthew 2:1–12

The Wise Men's Gifts

Gold, frankincense, and myrrh were very special gifts. The Wise Men gave these gifts to Jesus because they knew he was special. We can be like the Wise Men by making Jesus special in our lives too.

Jesus, Our Gift

Jesus is God's gift to us. He teaches us how to be gifts to others. We can do this by bringing Jesus' love into the world.

We can respect those who are not popular or rich. We can be friends to children who do not have many friends. We can bring cheer to someone who is ill. When we do these things, we are being gifts to others.

Give a Special Gift

Fill out the gift tag. Then on the lines below, tell about a gift of yourself that you will give someone this Christmas.

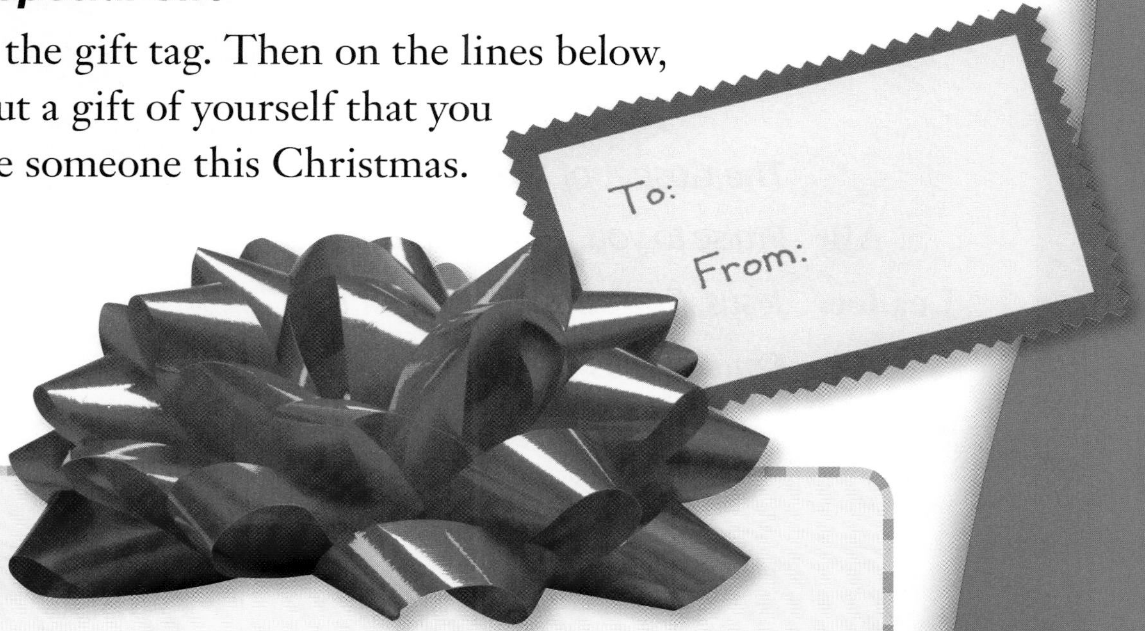

To:

From:

_____

_____

_____

_____

Prayer Service

Leader: *God gave us the greatest gift, his Son. Let us rejoice and adore Jesus, our Savior.*

Reader: *A reading from the holy Gospel according to Matthew.*

Bethlehem is a small town, but it is very important. A ruler will come from this town.

adapted from Matthew 2:6

The Gospel of the Lord.

All: *Praise to you, Lord Jesus Christ.*

Leader: *Jesus, God's Son, is born for us.*

All: *Come, let us adore him.*

Lent

Jesus loves little children. He tells his disciples to be like children.

Prayer

Jesus, my friend, teach me this Lent how to live as a child of God. I want to love God as you do.

Depending on Jesus

The disciples asked Jesus, "Who is the greatest in the
Kingdom of Heaven?" Jesus called a child to come join them.

He said, "You must become like this child. Then you will live
with God in Heaven."

adapted from Matthew 18:1–4

We Depend on God

Parents reach out to help their children. Children
depend on their parents and other adults who care for
them. We are all God's children. God reaches out to us.
We need God's help.

Making Changes

Jesus asked his disciples to change their lives. Lent is a time for change. We ask ourselves questions: How can I help others? How can I stay close to God? How can I be more like Jesus?

We receive ashes on our forehead on Ash Wednesday. This is when we tell God how we will change our lives during Lent. These ashes remind us that we follow Jesus.

Changing for the Better

What could you do to make the bad situations good? Draw a line to connect each box on the top row with its matching box on the bottom row.

Prayer Service

Leader: *Let us begin our prayer with the Sign of the Cross.*

Jesus taught us how to pray to God our Father. Let us tell Jesus that we will listen to him and follow him.

Reader: *A reading from the Book of Psalms.*

God loves those who hate evil. He protects those who are faithful. He rescues them from the wicked. If you are fair and honest, God will be with you.

adapted from Psalm 97:10–11

Leader: *Let us close by praying the Lord's Prayer together.*

Holy Week

Jesus was kind and loving to everyone. Jesus prayed for his enemies. How can you be like Jesus during Holy Week?

Prayer

Jesus, my helper, help me forgive those who hurt me.
I want to love others as you did.

Jesus' Great Love

Jesus was talking to his friends when a crowd arrived. A judge and his servant were part of the crowd. They came to arrest Jesus.

Jesus' friends rushed to help him. One of them cut the ear of the judge's servant. Jesus told his friend to stop. Jesus touched the servant's ear, and it was healed.

adapted from Luke 22:47–51

We Act Like Jesus

Jesus knew he would be arrested. Still, he reached out with a healing touch to his enemies. Jesus did not try to get even. He showed love instead.

We are called to be like Jesus. We are not to harm by word or deed those who do not like us. We can show love by praying for them and by being kind.

We Follow Jesus' Example

Write acts of love you will do during Holy Week to be like Jesus.

Prayer Service

Leader: *Jesus was a loving person even when he was about to be arrested. Let us listen to what Jesus tells us about loving others.*

Reader: *A reading from the holy Gospel according to Matthew.*

> You have heard people say, "You shall love your friend and hate your enemy." But I say that you should love your enemy. You should pray for those who hurt you. Then you will be children of God.

adapted from Matthew 5:43–45

The Gospel of the Lord.

All: *Praise to you, Lord Jesus Christ.*

Leader: *Let us remember that Jesus wants us to show his love as we pray the Sign of the Cross.*

Easter

Easter is a joyful time. We celebrate that Jesus is risen.

Prayer

Dear Jesus, help me be a person of joy. I want to help others be joyful too.

Looking for Jesus

Mary Magdalene and other women went to Jesus' tomb. They brought spices to put on his body. When they got there, the tomb was empty. An angel was there. The angel said to them, "Go and tell the disciples that Jesus is risen. He will meet them."

adapted from Mark 16:1–7

Meeting Jesus in Others

The women at the tomb were followers of Jesus. The angel's message meant that the disciples would meet Jesus in the people they would serve.

We meet Jesus in our lives when we help others. Who are the people we can love and serve?

Sunday, the Lord's Day

We celebrate the Resurrection on Sunday, the Lord's Day. On this day we remember that Jesus rose from the dead.

Loving and Serving Others

Write ways you love and serve others. These are ways you meet Jesus in your life.

_____

_____

_____

_____

_____

_____

_____

Prayer Service

Leader: *We meet Jesus in those we love and serve. We meet Jesus in a special way at Mass. Let us rejoice that the Lord is with us.*

A reading from the Book of Psalms.

Group A: Sing to the Lord a new song.

Group B: Sing to the Lord, all the earth.

Group A: Sing to the Lord and praise his name.

Group B: Sing day after day.

All: The Lord has saved us!

adapted from Psalm 96:1–2

Leader: *Let us continue to praise Jesus by loving one another.*

All: *Amen. Alleluia.*

Pentecost

The coming of the Holy Spirit is celebrated on Pentecost. The Holy Spirit came to Peter and the other disciples. They went out to tell everyone about Jesus.

Prayer

Jesus, teach me how to help others the way the disciples did.

Peter Helps

With the other disciples, Peter received the Holy Spirit on Pentecost. He wanted to tell people about Jesus.

Peter was going to the Temple to pray. He saw a poor man who could not walk. The man begged for money. Peter said, "I do not have silver or gold. What I do have, I will give you. In the name of Jesus Christ, get up and walk."

The man leaped up and walked around. He was very excited. He went into the Temple and praised God.

adapted from Acts of the Apostles 3:1–8

How did Peter's actions change the man's life?

What Can You Do?

Like Peter we have the help of the Holy Spirit. The Spirit leads us to pray and to care for others. Below each situation write what you could do to help the person in need.

1. Justin was absent from school. He needs help with his homework to catch up to the rest of the class.

   _____

   _____

2. Sara is crying. No one will help her learn how to ride her new bike.

   _____

   _____

3. Mona is feeling sad because the children at her new school do not include her.

   _____

   _____

4. Jimmy wants to be on the soccer team, but he does not know how to play.

   _____

   _____

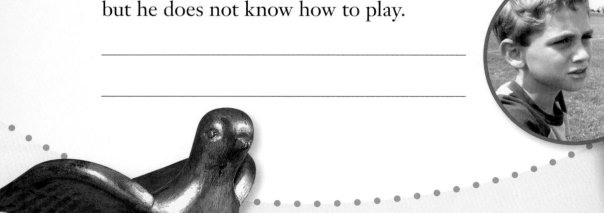

Prayer Service

Leader: *Peter called for Jesus' help in healing the man at the Temple. Let us pray that the Holy Spirit will lead us to serve others in Jesus' name.*

All: *Amen.*

Reader: *A reading from the letter of Saint Paul to the Galatians.*

When you help one another, you obey Jesus' law. Do not grow tired of doing good for others. You will be rewarded if you do not give up.

adapted from Galatians 6:2,9

The Word of the Lord.

All: *Thanks be to God.*

Leader: *Let us show our love for others every day.*

All Saints Day

On the Feast of All Saints, we remember the saints in Heaven. We want to become saints too. We want to live as children of God.

SANCTA CLARISSA

Prayer

Jesus, my brother, I want to follow you and be close to you.

Becoming Children of God

The people wanted to become children of God. So they asked Peter and Jesus' other disciples what they should do.

Peter said, "Be sorry for your sins and be baptized in the name of Jesus Christ. Your sins will be forgiven. You will receive the gift of the Holy Spirit. This promise is made for everyone God calls."

adapted from Acts of the Apostles 2:37–39

Living as God's Children

Jesus wants us to be close to him and to one another. He gives us the grace of the sacraments to help us. He asks us to pray for one another and for those who died. We ask the saints in Heaven to pray for us. We are all together in Jesus. This is the Communion of Saints.

Feast of All Saints

On November 1 we celebrate the Feast of All Saints. We go to Mass. We remember those who have died and now live with God.

It is also a good time to think about the special people in your life. Think of how they help you. Think of their good example. Think of their love for you.

In the frame draw a picture of one special person in your life. Write a sentence to tell why this person is special to you.

_____

_____

Prayer Service

Leader: *Jesus asks us to pray for one another.*

We pray for those who have died. Lord, have mercy on them.

All: *Lord, have mercy on them.*

Leader: *We ask the saints in Heaven to pray for us. Holy saints, help us to follow Jesus.*

All: *Holy saints, help us to follow Jesus.*

Reader: *A reading from the first letter of John.*

Beloved, we are God's children now.

adapted from I John 3:2

The Word of the Lord.

All: *Thanks be to God.*

Leader: *Let us close with the prayer to God the Father that Jesus taught us.*

Prayers and Practices of Our Faith

Knowing and Praying Our Faith

The Bible and You

God speaks to us in many ways. One way is through the Bible. The Bible is the story of God's promise to care for us, especially through his Son, Jesus.

The Bible is made up of two parts. The Old Testament tells stories about the Jewish people before Jesus was born.

In the New Testament, Jesus teaches us about the Father's love. The Gospels tell stories about Jesus' life, Death, and Resurrection.

At Mass we hear stories from the Bible. We can also read the Bible on our own.

Prayer and How We Pray

Prayer is talking and listening to God. We can talk to God in the words of special prayers or in our own words. We can pray aloud or quietly in our hearts.

We can pray to God often and in many different ways. We praise God. We can ask God for what we need and thank him. We can pray for ourselves and for others.

Prayers to Take to Heart

It is good for us to know prayers by heart. To take prayers to heart means that we not only learn, or memorize, the words but understand and live them.

Glory Be to the Father

Glory be to the Father,
and to the Son,
and to the Holy Spirit.
As it was in the beginning,
is now, and ever shall be,
world without end.
Amen.

Sign of the Cross

In the name of the Father,
and of the Son,
and of the Holy Spirit.
Amen.

Lord's Prayer

Our Father, who art in heaven,
hallowed be thy name;
thy kingdom come,
thy will be done
on earth as it is in heaven.
Give us this day our daily bread,
and forgive us our trespasses,
as we forgive those who trespass against us;
and lead us not into temptation,
but deliver us from evil.
Amen.

Hail Mary

Hail Mary, full of grace,
the Lord is with you.
Blessed are you among women,
and blessed is the fruit of your
*   womb, Jesus.*
Holy Mary, Mother of God,
pray for us sinners,
now and at the hour of
*   our death.*
Amen.

Act of Contrition

My God,
I am sorry for my sins with all my heart.
In choosing to do wrong
and failing to do good,
I have sinned against you
whom I should love above all things.
I firmly intend, with your help,
to do penance,
to sin no more,
and to avoid whatever leads me to sin.
Our Savior Jesus Christ
suffered and died for us.
In his name, my God, have mercy.

Prayer to the Holy Spirit

Come, Holy Spirit, fill the hearts of your faithful.
And kindle in them the fire of your love.
Send forth your Spirit and they shall be created.
And you will renew the face of the earth.
Let us pray.

Lord,
by the light of the Holy Spirit
you have taught the hearts of your faithful.
In the same Spirit
help us to relish what is right
and always rejoice in your consolation.
We ask this through Christ our Lord.
Amen.

Morning Prayer

God, our Father, I offer you today
All that I think and do and say.
I offer it with what was done on earth
By Jesus Christ, your Son.
Amen.

Evening Prayer

God, our Father, this day is done.
We ask you and Jesus Christ, your Son,
that with the Spirit, our welcome guest,
you guard our sleep and bless our rest.
Amen.

Prayer Before Meals

Bless us, O Lord, and these your gifts
which we are about to receive from your goodness.
Through Christ our Lord.
Amen.

Prayer After Meals

We give you thanks
for all your gifts,
almighty God,
living and reigning
now and for ever.
Amen.

Apostles' Creed

I believe in God,
the Father almighty,
Creator of heaven and earth,
and in Jesus Christ, his only Son, our Lord,
who was conceived by the Holy Spirit,
born of the Virgin Mary,
suffered under Pontius Pilate,
was crucified, died and was buried;
he descended into hell;
on the third day he rose again from the dead;
he ascended into heaven,
and is seated at the right hand of God
the Father almighty;
from there he will come to judge the living
and the dead.

I believe in the Holy Spirit,
the holy catholic Church,
the communion of saints,
the forgiveness of sins,
the resurrection of the body,
and life everlasting. Amen.

Hail, Holy Queen (*Salve Regina*)

Hail, holy Queen, Mother of mercy,
hail, our life, our sweetness, and our hope.
To you we cry, the children of Eve;
to you we send up our sighs,
mourning and weeping in this land of exile.
Turn, then, most gracious advocate,
your eyes of mercy toward us;
lead us home at last
and show us the blessed
   fruit of your womb, Jesus:
O clement, O loving,
   O sweet Virgin Mary.

Prayer for Vocations

God, thank you for loving me.
You have called me
to live as your child.
Help all your children
to love you and one another.
Amen.

The Rosary

Praying the Rosary helps us reflect on the special events, or mysteries, in the lives of Jesus and Mary. These steps will help you learn to pray the Rosary.

1. Begin by praying the Sign of the Cross while holding the crucifix. Then pray the Apostles' Creed.

2. Hold the first single bead and pray the Lord's Prayer.

3. On each of the next three beads, pray a Hail Mary. End with one Glory Be to the Father.

4. On the next single bead, think about the first mystery, a particular event in the lives of Jesus and Mary. Then pray the Lord's Prayer.

5. On the next ten beads, pray a Hail Mary as you hold each bead. Each set of ten beads is called a decade. As you pray the decade, reflect on the first mystery. At the end of the decade, pray the Glory Be to the Father.

6–13. Pray the four remaining decades in the same way, using the single bead between each set to pray the Lord's Prayer. Think about a different mystery each time.

   Many people pray the Hail, Holy Queen after the last decade.

14. End by praying the Sign of the Cross while holding the crucifix.

Praying the Rosary

9. Pray ten Hail Marys and one Glory Be to the Father.

10. Think about the fourth mystery. Pray the Lord's Prayer.

11. Pray ten Hail Marys and one Glory Be to the Father.

8. Think about the third mystery. Pray the Lord's Prayer.

7. Pray ten Hail Marys and one Glory Be to the Father.

12. Think about the fifth mystery. Pray the Lord's Prayer.

6. Think about the second mystery. Pray the Lord's Prayer.

5. Pray ten Hail Marys and one Glory Be to the Father.

13. Pray ten Hail Marys and one Glory Be to the Father.

4. Think about the first mystery. Pray the Lord's Prayer.

Pray the Hail, Holy Queen.
Many people pray the Hail, Holy Queen after the last decade.

3. Pray three Hail Marys and one Glory Be to the Father.

2. Pray the Lord's Prayer.

14. Pray the Sign of the Cross.

1. Pray the Sign of the Cross and the Apostles' Creed.

Celebrating Our Faith

The Seven Sacraments

The sacraments are ways in which God enters our lives.

Sacraments show that God is part of our lives. Jesus gave them to the Church to show that he loves us. The seven sacraments help us live the way God wants us to live. Priests celebrate the sacraments with us.

Baptism

Baptism is the first sacrament we receive. Through Baptism we become followers of Jesus and part of God's family, the Church.

The pouring of water is the main sign of Baptism. Along with Confirmation and the Eucharist, Baptism is a Sacrament of Initiation.

Confirmation

Confirmation is a Sacrament of Initiation.

In this sacrament the Holy Spirit strengthens us to be witnesses to Jesus. Confirmation makes us stronger in faith and helps us become better Christians.

The bishop places holy oil in the form of a cross on our foreheads. This is the main sign of Confirmation.

Eucharist

The Eucharist is a Sacrament of Initiation.

At Mass the bread and wine become the Body and Blood of Jesus Christ. This happens when the priest says the words of consecration that Jesus used at the Last Supper. The Eucharist is also called Holy Communion.

Reconciliation

We ask God to forgive our sins in the Sacrament of Penance and Reconciliation. The priest who celebrates this sacrament with us shares Jesus' gifts of peace and forgiveness.

God always forgives us when we are sorry and do penance for our sins.

Anointing of the Sick

In this sacrament a sick person is anointed with holy oil and receives the spiritual—and sometimes even physical—healing of Jesus.

Holy Orders

Some men are called to be deacons, priests, or bishops. They receive the Sacrament of Holy Orders. Through Holy Orders the mission, or task, given by Jesus to his apostles continues in the Church.

Matrimony

Some men and women are called to be married. In the Sacrament of Matrimony, they make a solemn promise to be partners for life, both for their own good and for the good of the children they will raise.

Celebrating the Lord's Day

Sunday is the day on which we celebrate the Resurrection of Jesus. Sunday is the Lord's Day. We gather for Mass and rest from work. People all over the world gather at God's eucharistic table as brothers and sisters.

The Order of Mass

The Mass is the most important sacramental celebration of the Church, and it always follows a set order.

Introductory Rites—
preparing to celebrate
the Eucharist

Entrance Chant

We gather as a community
and praise God in song.

Greeting

We pray the Sign of the Cross.
The priest welcomes us.

Penitential Act

We remember our sins and ask God for mercy.

Gloria

We praise God in song.

Collect Prayer

We ask God to hear our prayers.

Liturgy of the Word—
hearing God's plan
of Salvation

First Reading

We listen to God's Word,
usually from the Old
Testament.

Responsorial Psalm

We respond to God's Word
in song.

Second Reading

We listen to God's Word from
the New Testament.

Gospel Acclamation

We sing "Alleluia!" to praise God for the Good News.
During Lent we use a different acclamation.

Gospel Reading

We stand and listen to the Gospel of the Lord.

Homily

The priest or deacon explains God's Word.

Profession of Faith

We proclaim our faith through the Creed.

Prayer of the Faithful

We pray for our needs and the needs of others.

Liturgy of the Eucharist—
celebrating Jesus Christ's presence in the Eucharist

Presentation and Preparation of the Gifts

We bring gifts of bread and wine to the altar.

Prayer over the Offerings

The priest prays that God will accept our sacrifice.

Eucharistic Prayer

This prayer of thanksgiving is the center and high point of the entire celebration. During this prayer the bread and wine truly become the Body and Blood of Jesus Christ.

Communion Rite—preparing to receive the Body and Blood of Jesus Christ

The Lord's Prayer

We pray the Lord's Prayer.

Sign of Peace

We offer one another Christ's peace.

Lamb of God

We pray the Lamb of God and ask for forgiveness, mercy, and peace.

Communion

We receive the Body and Blood of Jesus Christ.

Concluding Rites—going forth in peace

Final Blessing

We receive God's blessing.

Dismissal

We go in peace to glorify the Lord by our lives.

Receiving Holy Communion

When we receive Holy Communion, we receive the Body of Christ—in the form of bread—in our hands or on our tongues. The priest or the extraordinary minister of Holy Communion says, "The Body of Christ." We reply, "Amen."

We can also receive the Blood of Christ—in the form of wine. The priest or the extraordinary minister of Holy Communion offers the chalice and says, "The Blood of Christ." We reply, "Amen." We take the chalice in our hands and drink from it, and we then hand it back to the priest or extraordinary minister of Holy Communion.

Holy Days of Obligation

Holy Days of Obligation are the days other than Sundays on which Catholics gather for Mass to celebrate the great things God has done for us through Jesus and the saints.

Six Holy Days of Obligation are celebrated in the United States.

January 1—Mary, Mother of God

40 days after Easter—Ascension

August 15—Assumption of the Blessed Virgin Mary

November 1—All Saints Day

December 8—Immaculate Conception

December 25—Nativity of Our Lord Jesus Christ

People and Things I See at Mass

alb

altar server

sanctuary lamp

processional cross

Paschal Candle

tabernacle

ambo

altar servers

extraordinary minister of Holy Communion

stole

chasuble

deacon

priest

lector

cantor

altar

chalice

paten

An Examination of Conscience

An examination of conscience is the act of reflecting on how we have hurt our relationships with God and others. Questions such as the following will help us in our examination of conscience.

My Relationship with God

Do I use God's name with love and reverence?

What steps am I taking to grow closer to God and to others?

Do I actively participate at Mass on Sundays and Holy Days of Obligation?

Do I pray?

My Relationships with Family, Friends, and Neighbors

Have I set a bad example by my words or actions? Do I treat others fairly?

Am I loving to those in my family? Am I respectful of my neighbors, my friends, and those in authority?

Do I show respect for my body and for the bodies of others?

Have I taken or damaged anything that did not belong to me? Have I cheated or lied?

Do I quarrel or fight with others? Do I try to hurt people who I think have hurt me?

How to Go to Confession

An examination of conscience is an important part of preparing for the Sacrament of Reconciliation. The Sacrament of Reconciliation includes the following steps.

1. The priest greets us, and we pray the Sign of the Cross. He invites us to trust in God. He may read God's Word with us.

2. We confess our sins. The priest may help and counsel us.

3. The priest gives us a penance to perform. Penance may be an act of kindness or prayers to pray, or both.

4. The priest asks us to express our sorrow, usually by praying the Act of Contrition.

5. We receive absolution. The priest says, "I absolve you from your sins in the name of the Father, and of the Son, and of the Holy Spirit." We respond, "Amen."

6. The priest dismisses us by saying, "Go in peace." We go forth to perform the act of penance he has given us.

Living Our Faith

The Ten Commandments

God gave us the Ten Commandments. They teach us how to live for God and for others. They help us follow the moral law to do good and avoid evil.

1. I am your God; love nothing more than me.
2. Use God's name with respect.
3. Keep the Lord's Day holy.
4. Honor and obey your parents.
5. Treat all human life with respect.
6. Respect married life.
7. Respect what belongs to others.
8. Tell the truth.
9. Respect your neighbors and your friends.
10. Be happy with what you have.

The Great Commandment

People asked Jesus, "What is the most important commandment?" Jesus said, "First, love God. Love him with your heart, soul, and mind. The second is like it: Love your neighbor as much as you love yourself."

adapted from Matthew 22:37–39

We call this the Great Commandment.

The New Commandment

Before his Death on the cross, Jesus gave his disciples a new commandment.

"[L]ove one another. As I have loved you, so you also should love one another."

John 13:34

The Beatitudes

Jesus gave us the Beatitudes in the Sermon on the Mount. They show us the way to true happiness.

Blessed are those who are kind to others. They will be rewarded.

Blessed are those who do the right thing even when it is difficult. They will be with God one day.

Blessed are those who are fair to others. They will be treated fairly.

Blessed are those who work for peace. They are God's children.

adapted from Matthew 5:1–10

Making Good Choices

The Holy Spirit helps us make good choices. We get help from the Ten Commandments, the grace of the sacraments, and the teachings of the Church. We also get help from the example of the saints and fellow Christians. To make good choices, we ask the following questions:

1. Is the thing I am choosing to do a good thing?

2. Am I choosing to do it for the right reasons?

3. Am I choosing to do it at the right time and in the right place?

Fruits of the Holy Spirit

When we realize that the Holy Spirit lives within us, we live the way God wants us to. The Fruits of the Holy Spirit are signs of the Holy Spirit's action in our lives. They include the following.

love	generosity	peace
kindness	faithfulness	patience
gentleness	self-control	joy

Church Tradition also includes **goodness, modesty,** and **chastity** among the Fruits of the Holy Spirit.

Showing Our Love for the World

Jesus taught us to care for those in need. The Social Teachings of the Church call us to follow Jesus' example in each of the following areas.

Life and Dignity

God wants us to care for everyone. We are all made in his image.

Family and Community

Jesus wants us to be loving helpers in our families and communities.

Rights and Responsibilities

All people should have what they need to live good lives.

The Poor and Vulnerable

Jesus calls us to do what we can to help people in need.

Work and Workers

The work that we do gives glory to God.

Solidarity

Since God is our Father, we are called to treat everyone in the world as a brother or a sister.

God's Creation

We show our love for God's world by taking care of it.

Songs of Our Faith

Song of Love

Chorus

Thank you, Jesus,
    for helping me to see.
Thank you, God,
    for the heart you've given me.
Thank you, Spirit,
    for coming to me,
and for showing me how to sing
    your song of love.

Verse 1

I saw someone lonely by the road,
someone my age sadly all alone.
I shared my friendship, and we talked a while.
I gave my hand. Jesus gave back a smile.

(Sing Chorus)

Verse 2

I saw Jesus inside my heart,
making me God's own work of art.
If I spread my joy in life each day,
I can show my love for God's world in every way.

(Sing Chorus)

Verse 3

I saw Jesus in friends and family
by my side, sharing and supporting me.
I found my heart had room for everyone.
Thank you, Spirit, for what you have begun.

(Sing Chorus)

Lyrics by E. Strauss. Music by Neilson Hubbard.
© 2005 Loyola Press. All rights reserved.

"Echo" Holy, Holy

Verse 1

Holy, Holy, Holy, (Holy, Holy, Holy)
Lord, God of power and might; (Lord, God
   of power and might)
Heaven, heaven and earth (Heaven, heaven and earth)
are full of your glory. (are full of your glory)

Chorus

Sing Hosanna, (sing Hosanna,)
sing Hosanna, (sing Hosanna,)
sing Hosanna, (sing Hosanna,)
sing alleluia. (sing alleluia.)

Verse 2

Blessed, blessed is he, (Blessed, blessed is he,)
who comes in the name of the Lord.
   (who comes in the name of the Lord.)

(Sing Chorus)

Jesus in the Morning
(Jesus Verses)

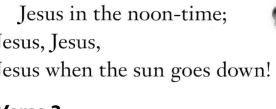

Verse 1

Jesus, Jesus,
Jesus in the morning,
    Jesus in the noon-time;
Jesus, Jesus,
Jesus when the sun goes down!

Verse 2

Praise him, praise him,
Praise him in the morning, praise him in the noon-time;
Praise him, praise him,
Praise him when the sun goes down!

Verse 3

Love him, love him,
Love him in the morning, love him in the noon-time;
Love him, love him,
Love him when the sun goes down!

Verse 4

Jesus, Jesus,
Jesus in the morning, Jesus in noon-time;
Jesus, Jesus,
Jesus when the sun goes down!

*"Jesus in the Morning" text and tune from
traditional African American folk song.*

Our Father

Our Father,
who art in heaven,
hallowed be thy name;
thy kingdom come;
thy will be done on earth as it is in heaven.
Give us this day our daily bread;
and forgive us our trespasses
as we forgive those who trespass against us;
and lead us not into temptation,
but deliver us from evil.
Amen.

"Our Father" tune from traditional chant.

Jesus in the Morning
(Spirit Verses)

Verse 1

Spirit, Spirit,
Spirit in the morning, Spirit in
 the noon-time;
Spirit, Spirit,
Spirit when the sun goes down!

Verse 2

Calls me, calls me,
Calls me in the morning, calls me in
 the noon-time;
Calls me, calls me,
Calls me when the sun goes down!

Verse 3

Loves me, loves me,
Loves me in the morning, loves me in the noon-time;
Loves me, loves me,
Loves me when the sun goes down!

Verse 4

Spirit, Spirit,
Spirit in the morning, Spirit in noon-time;
Spirit, Spirit,
Spirit when the sun goes down!

*"Jesus in the Morning" text and tune from
traditional African American folk song.*

A Man Named Zacchaeus

Verse 1

A man named Zacchaeus from old Jericho
came out to see Jesus one day long ago.
Zacchaeus was short, but he wanted to see.
So up, up he climbed in a sycamore tree.
Zacchaeus was short, but he wanted to see.
So up, up he climbed in a sycamore tree.

Verse 2

Zacchaeus was wealthy while others were poor.
They all got less but Zacchaeus got more.
"Come down, Zacchaeus," said Jesus, "Come down.
I'll be your friend, but you must turn around."
"Come down, Zacchaeus," said Jesus, "Come down.
I'll be your friend, but you must turn around."

Verse 3

Zacchaeus came down and he changed on that day.
Zacchaeus gave half of his money away.
Now he's the happiest person in town.
Zacchaeus was lost, but now he is found.
Now he's the happiest person in town.
Zacchaeus was lost, but now he is found.

Verse 4

Now Jesus is travelling to our town today.
So what should we do to prepare him a way?
Feed all the hungry and care for the poor,
then Jesus will stay with us forever more.
Feed all the hungry and care for the poor,
then Jesus will stay with us forever more.

"A Man Named Zacchaeus" by Jack Miffleton. © 1990 North American Liturgy Resources. 5536 NE Hassalo, Portland, OR 97213. All rights reserved. Used with permission.

Friends, All Gather 'Round

Refrain

Friends, all gather 'round the table of the Lord.
Friends, all gather 'round the table of the Lord. (Repeat)

Verse 1

As friends we gather for friends we have become.
Friends, all gather 'round the table of the Lord.

(Sing Refrain)

Verse 2

Join in the feast of joy, the banquet table of love.
Friends, all gather 'round the table of the Lord.

(Sing Refrain)

Verse 3

Singing in praise of God the giver of good gifts.
Friends, all gather 'round the table of the Lord.

(Sing Refrain)

"Friends, All Gather 'Round" by Carey Landry.
© 1979 North American Liturgy Resources.
5536 NE Hassalo, Portland, OR 97213.
All rights reserved. Used with permission.

Jesus, Jesus

Verse 1

Jesus, Jesus,
let us tell you how we feel.
You have made your home within us,
we love you so.

Verse 2

Jesus, Jesus,
let us tell you how we feel.
You have given us your forgiveness,
we love you so.

Verse 3

Jesus, Jesus,
Let us tell you how we feel.
You have given us your mercy,
we love you so.

You have given us your mercy,
we love you so.

We Come to Your Table

Verse 1

Gentle Jesus, risen Lord,
we come to your table;
with our hearts so full of joy,
we come to your table.

Refrain

We come, we come,
we come to your table.
We come, we come,
we come to your table.

Verse 2

In your body we find life,
we come to your table;
life you give for us to share,
we come to your table.

(Sing Refrain)

Verse 3

Jesus Savior, living bread!
We come to your table;
Bread of heaven, bread of hope,
We come to your table.

(Sing Refrain)

Verse 4

You invite us, we rejoice!
We come to your table;
We remember, we give thanks!
We come to your table.

(Sing Refrain)

*"We Come to Your Table" by Carey Landry.
© 1973 North American Liturgy Resources.
5536 NE Hassalo, Portland, OR 97213.
All rights reserved. Used with permission.*

Jesus' Hands Were Kind Hands

Verse 1

Jesus' hands were kind hands,
    doing good to all,
Healing pain and sickness,
    blessing children small.
Washing tired feet and saving
    those who fall,
Jesus' hands were kind hands,
    doing good to all.

Verse 2

Take my hands, Lord Jesus, let them work for you;
Make them strong and gentle, kind in all I do.
Let me watch you, Jesus, till I'm gentle too,
Till my hands are kind hands, quick to work for you.

Verse 3

Jesus' hands were kind hands, doing good to all,
Healing pain and sickness, blessing children small.
Washing tired feet and saving those who fall;
Jesus' hands were kind hands, doing good to all.

Verse 4

Take my hands, Lord Jesus, let them work for you;
Make them strong and gentle, kind in all I do.
Let me watch you, Jesus, till I'm gentle too,
Till my hands are kind hands, quick to work for you.

This Little Light of Mine

Verse 1

This little light of mine,
I'm gonna let it shine.
This little light of mine,
I'm gonna let it shine.
This little light of mine,
I'm gonna let it shine.
Let it shine,
let it shine,
let it shine.

Verse 2

Everywhere I go,
I'm gonna let it shine.
Everywhere I go,
I'm gonna let it shine.
Everywhere I go,
I'm gonna let it shine.
Let it shine,
let it shine,
let it shine.

Verse 3

Jesus gave it to me,
I'm gonna let it shine.
Jesus gave it to me,
I'm gonna let it shine.
Jesus gave it to me,
I'm gonna let it shine.
Let it shine,
let it shine,
let it shine.

"This Little Light of Mine" text and tune from traditional African American spiritual.

Name _____   Date _____

Art Print 1 shows God's creatures of the air, land, and sea. How is God's creation a gift to us? How can we care for God's creation?

God Made Heaven and Earth

At first, there was only God—the Father, the Son, and the Holy Spirit.

God made the world. He made the sky, the sun, and the moon. He made the sea. God filled it with different kinds of fish. He made the land. He filled it with many kinds of animals.

Then God said, "Let us make someone special." So God made a man and a woman. He blessed them and told them to have children. He told them to take good care of the earth.

God looked at everything he had made. God was pleased with all he had done.

adapted from Genesis 1:1–31

Taking Care of God's Earth

God created the sky, land, sea, and animals. Like the first man and woman, God wants us to take care of the earth. How do you show your family and friends that you take care of God's creation? Write one thing you do. Write one thing you see others do.

_____

_____

Name _____   Date _____

Art Print 2 shows a colorful picture of the Holy Family.
What do you like to do with your family?

The Story of Joseph

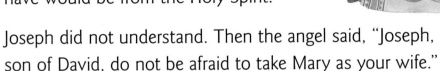

Before Joseph and Mary were married, an angel appeared to Joseph in a dream. The angel told Joseph that the baby that Mary was going to have would be from the Holy Spirit.

Joseph did not understand. Then the angel said, "Joseph, son of David, do not be afraid to take Mary as your wife."

The angel told Joseph to name the child Jesus. The name *Jesus* means "God saves" or "God saves us." Because Jesus saves us from our sins, he is our **Savior.**

After Joseph woke up from his dream, he took Mary as his wife.

adapted from Matthew 1:18–24

Families Are Special

Like the Holy Family, every member of your family is important. This makes your family special. Write two ways that tell how your family is special.

_____

_____

_____

_____

Reading God's Word

I will be with you always, until the end of the world!

adapted from Matthew 28:20

Name _____ Date _____

Art Print 3 shows a playful view of the earth from space. How does God care for the earth and for us?

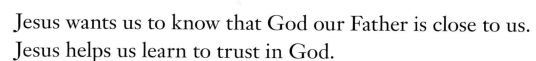

Trust in God

Jesus wants us to know that God our Father is close to us. Jesus helps us learn to trust in God.

Jesus said, "Do not worry about your life. Do not worry about what you will eat or drink or what you will wear. Worrying will not add one minute to your life."

"See the birds that fly and the flowers that grow. The birds in the sky do not work. Yet God gives them the food they need to live."

"Be like the flowers that grow wild. They do not work. But God helps them grow strong. God provides for all of them. And he will provide for you."

adapted from Matthew 6:25–34

Resting in God's Hands

When you trust in God, you feel as if you are being held in his hands. Close your eyes. Imagine being held by God. How does it feel? Write your feelings.

_____

_____

_____

Reading God's Word

Trust in the power of God. Place all your cares in his hands because he cares for you.   *adapted from 1 Peter 5:6–7*

Name _____ Date _____

Art Print 4 shows Jesus bringing light to a dark world.
How can you bring the light of the Holy Spirit to those around you?

The Work of the Holy Spirit

We learn about the goodness of Jesus through the Holy Spirit. The Holy Spirit works within us and helps us do good things. We should not hide the good things we do. When others see the good we do, we shine like a light to the world.

Jesus said, "You are the light of the world. You cannot hide a city on a hill. No one lights a lamp and puts it under a basket. The lamp is put on a lamp stand. There it can give light to everyone in the house. Let your light shine on everyone you know. This way they will see the good things you do. Then they will praise God, the Father, in heaven."

adapted from Matthew 5:14–16

Shine a Light on Good Deeds

When we do good things, we know the Holy Spirit is helping us. Write a good thing you have done for others. Write a good thing that someone has done for you.

_____

_____

_____

_____

Reading God's Word

You will be my light to the ends of the earth so that all people may be saved.   *adapted from Isaiah 49:6*

Name _____   Date _____

Art Print 5 shows the breaking of the bread at Mass.
What is your favorite part of the Mass?

We Celebrate Ordinary Time

During Ordinary Time we celebrate Jesus. We learn to listen to his message and follow his example.

Green is the color of Ordinary Time. It is also the color of nature when everything grows. We grow in Ordinary Time also. We grow by learning more about Jesus. We grow by showing our love for Jesus and others. It is a good time to reflect on all that is good and turn what we have learned into action.

Mass in Ordinary Time

When we go to Mass, we see the priest wearing a green **chasuble.** The chasuble is the outermost layer of a priest's vestments worn when celebrating Mass.

Color this chasuble green as a symbol of Ordinary Time.

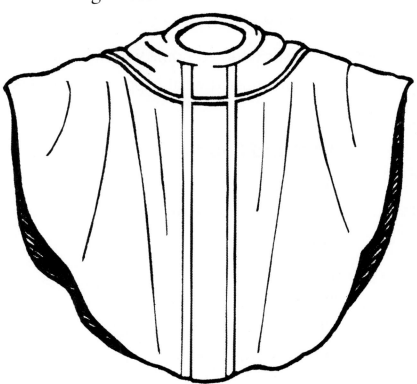

Name _____ Date _____

Art Print 6 shows Jesus talking to the teachers.
What do you talk about with your teachers?

Jesus with the Teachers

When Jesus was 12 years old, he went with his parents to a festival in Jerusalem. After the festival Mary and Joseph headed for home with their friends. Mary and Joseph thought Jesus was traveling with them. When they could not find him, they became very worried. Mary and Joseph returned to Jerusalem to look for Jesus. After three days they found him in the Temple.

Jesus was sitting with the teachers, listening to them and asking questions. When his parents saw him, they were amazed.

Mary asked, "Son, why did you do this to us? We were very worried about you."

Jesus said, "I must do what my Father wants me to do." His parents did not completely understand.

Jesus returned home with Mary and Joseph. Mary remembered what happened. Jesus grew older and wiser.

adapted from Luke 2:41–52

Lost and Found

Think of a time you lost something special. Draw a picture of how you felt when it was lost and how you felt when it was found.

Lost	Found

Name _____   Date _____

Art Print 7 shows Jesus healing a blind man. People talked about Jesus' miracles. What do you tell others about Jesus?

Jesus Heals

Jesus helped many people who were in need. He gave sight to those who could not see. He healed people who could not walk. These are examples of Jesus' **miracles.**

At the same time, there was a holy man named John the Baptist. He was teaching people about the coming of the Messiah. Some of John's followers told him about Jesus. So John sent them to ask Jesus, "Are you the one we are waiting for, or should we keep looking?"

Jesus said to John's followers, "Go and tell John what you have seen and heard. The blind see again. The sick get well. The deaf hear, and the dead are raised. The poor hear the good news that God loves them.

adapted from Luke 7:18–22

Love Through Actions

Think about ways you can be like Jesus by helping people. Write two things you can do to help others.

_____

_____

Reading God's Word

The eyes of the blind and the ears of the deaf will be opened.

adapted from Isaiah 35:5

Name _____   Date _____

Art Print 8 shows the parable of the banquet. How does God welcome everyone? How do we welcome others?

The Parable of the Banquet

Jesus often told a **parable,** or story, to teach an important lesson. This parable tells how everyone is invited to follow God.

A man planned a dinner party and invited many people. On the day of the party, the man sent his servant to tell the guests, "Come, everything is ready."

One by one, the guests made excuses. One said, "Sorry, but I must check the new land I bought." Another said, "I must take care of the animals I bought."

The servant reported to the master who got very angry. He said, "Go into the town. Bring the poor and the sick, the blind and the lame." Even so, there was still room for more guests.

The master said, "Go out to the streets and highways. Have people come and fill my house."

adapted from Luke 14:16–23

God's Invitation

Write a note thanking God for his invitation to be close to him.

Art Print 9 shows a sculpture of Jesus as the Good Shepherd. How are you a good shepherd at home or school?

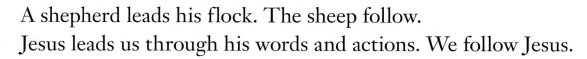

Jesus, Our Shepherd

A shepherd cares for his sheep.
Jesus cares for us.

A shepherd leads his flock. The sheep follow.
Jesus leads us through his words and actions. We follow Jesus.

A shepherd searches for any sheep that stray.
Jesus will always help us come back to him.

A shepherd feeds his flock.
Jesus feeds us through the Eucharist.

The Good Shepherd

Draw a picture of Jesus as your shepherd.

Name _____   Date _____

Art Print 10 shows an Advent wreath.
How does Jesus light our way?

Lighting the Way for Jesus

Advent is a time of waiting and getting ready to celebrate the birth of Jesus. Advent is also a time of lights. We see lighted candles on the Advent wreath. Homes and trees are decorated with colorful lights.

Lights remind us that Jesus lights our way to love and happiness. We can do many things to make room for Jesus' light in our hearts. We can pray. We can do good deeds. We can enjoy family customs to remember the true meaning of Christmas.

Making Room for Jesus' Light

Write a list of specific things you will do this Advent to make room for the light of Jesus. Then draw a picture that shows how you feel when the waiting is over and Christmas has come.

Things I Can Do This Advent

_____

_____

_____

_____

_____

_____

Art Print 11 shows a beautiful flowering tree. What beautiful things are growing in you as you grow closer to God?

Jesus Is the Vine

Take a walk. Look at the branches on trees. The healthy branches are like people who live close to God. God helps us when we invite him into our lives. We can ask God to guide us.

> Jesus said, "I am the vine, and my Father is the vine grower. He helps the good branches become healthier. You are already healthy because you have listened to what I have said."
>
> Jesus continued, "A branch cannot grow strong unless it stays on the vine. You cannot grow strong unless you stay close to me. Whoever stays close to me will grow strong."
>
> *adapted from John 15:1–5*

Grow Like a Vine

Write two ways you can grow closer to God.

_____

_____

Reading God's Word

The fruit of the Spirit is love, joy, peace, patience, and kindness.

adapted from Galatians 5:22

Name _____ Date _____

Art Print 12 shows Jesus talking with a man who is in a tree.
What would you like to talk with Jesus about today?

Zacchaeus, the Rich Man

Zacchaeus was a dishonest tax collector. He was very rich.
One day he heard that Jesus was coming through town.
Zacchaeus wanted to see Jesus very much. But Jesus
was walking in a big crowd, and Zacchaeus was
not tall. He could not see over the crowd.

Zacchaeus ran ahead and climbed up a tree.
Jesus saw him and said, "Zacchaeus, come down. I want to
stay at your house today." This made Zacchaeus very happy.

The people in the crowd became angry. They wondered why
Jesus was going to the home of a sinner.

Zacchaeus said to Jesus, "I will give half of everything I have
to the poor. I will give money back to anyone I have cheated."

Jesus was pleased. He said that Zacchaeus was saved that day.

adapted from Luke 19:2–9

Forgive One Another

Jesus forgave Zacchaeus. Write what forgiveness means to you.

Forgiveness means _____

_____ .

Reading God's Word

Sell what you have and give to those who do not have much.
Your treasure is with the Lord. No thief can steal that from you.

adapted from Luke 12:33

Name _____   Date _____

Art Print 13 shows four friends lowering a man through the roof. How would you help a friend who wanted to see Jesus?

Jesus Heals

Jesus was talking with some people in a house. The people crowded the rooms and blocked the doorways.

Four men came carrying their friend who wanted to see Jesus. He was paralyzed and could not walk. The men climbed to the roof and made an opening. They lowered their friend to Jesus.

Jesus saw their faith. He said to the man who was paralyzed, "Your sins are forgiven." Some people said, "Only God can forgive sins!"

Jesus told the people that he had the power to forgive sins. He turned to the man who was paralyzed and said, "Stand up and walk home." The man got up and walked away. The people were amazed. They knew that Jesus must be God.

adapted from Mark 2:1–12

Friendship

Draw a picture of a time that you helped a friend. Write one word on the line below that describes how you felt afterward.

_____

Name _____   Date _____

Art Print 14 shows the Virgin Mary with flowers.
If you could give Mary a gift, what would it be?

Mother of the Church

Like Mary, the Church has a special
relationship with God.

The Church is made up of people who are
called by God. The Church shows how much
God loves the world. God loves everyone.

Mary is the Mother of the Church.
She received God's help to follow him.

God gives us the same help,
or grace. Mary prays for us
so that we will listen to God.

Special Women

Mary is a special woman in
our faith. Draw a picture
of a special woman in your
life. Write three words that
describe her.

_____

_____

_____

Reading God's Word

Mary remembered all these things and kept them always
in her heart.

adapted from Luke 2:19

Name _____ Date _____

Art Print 15 shows the manger scene in Bethlehem.
Imagine yourself at the manger. Where would you like to be?

The Feast of Christmas

The feast of Christmas celebrates the mystery of Jesus' birth.

Christmas is a time to celebrate with our families. It is a time to share with friends. Families and friends gather in church to celebrate the birth of Jesus.

Christmas is also a time for giving. God gave his only Son to us. When you look at a Nativity scene, remember God's greatest gift as you observe Mary, Joseph, and the baby Jesus.

Gifts from family and friends are given and unwrapped at Christmas. You are a gift as well. Unwrap your talents and share them with others for Christmas.

You Are a Gift

Write a list of talents you can unwrap for Christmas to share with others.

_____

_____

_____

_____

_____

_____

_____

Name _____ Date _____

Art Print 16 shows Saint Peter holding two keys.
In what ways are you a leader?

Peter Speaks to the People

Jesus chose Peter to lead the Church. He wanted Peter
to keep showing people how to be close to God.

> Peter said to the people, "Change your lives and be baptized
> in the name of Jesus Christ. Then your sins will be forgiven.
> You will receive the gift of the Holy Spirit."
>
> *adapted from Acts of the Apostles 2:38*

Saint Peter Is a Leader

A leader is not the first or the greatest
person. A leader is someone who serves others.
A leader helps others become the best they can be.

Cut out and glue pictures of leaders below. Look in newspapers
or magazines. They can be school, Church, community, state,
country, or world leaders. Say a prayer for them each day.

© LOYOLA PRESS.

Name _____ Date _____

Art Print 17 shows adults and children walking to a country church. How do you get ready to go to Mass?

We Are Members of the Church

Followers of Jesus make others feel welcome inside of church. When you go to Mass, you gather with others to worship. When you leave, your work is not done. You continue the work of Jesus. People who worship in a parish also give their time and talents to serve others. This is called a **ministry**. Ministry is service or work done for others.

List what you do inside church as a follower of Jesus. Then list what you do outside of church. Write your ideas in the chart.

In Church	Outside of Church
_____	_____
_____	_____
_____	_____
_____	_____
_____	_____
_____	_____

Link to Liturgy

Many churches have ministers of hospitality who welcome people to the parish church for Mass.

Name _____ Date _____

Art Print 18 shows a plaque with symbols of the four Gospel writers.
If you were a Gospel writer, what would you write about Jesus?

The Four Gospels

MATTHEW

At Mass we listen to God's Word in the Bible.
When it is time for the Liturgy of the Word, what
do you see and hear? The priest or deacon reads
from the *Lectionary for Mass.* He reads a story
about Jesus' life from one of the four Gospels.
It is one part of the Liturgy of the Word.

MARK

The Gospels are from a part of the Bible called
the New Testament. The Gospel writers are
Matthew, Mark, Luke, and John. They are
called **Evangelists.**

The Evangelists are often shown as symbols.
Matthew is a winged man. Mark is a winged lion.
Luke is a winged ox. John is an eagle.

LUKE

Symbol Match

Think about the meaning for each symbol.
Draw a line from each symbol to its meaning.

JOHN

1. winged man ●

2. winged lion ●

3. winged ox ●

4. eagle ●

● **a.** strength, sacrifice

● **b.** swift, Heaven

● **c.** human, thinking

● **d.** courage, royalty

Name _____ Date _____

Art Print 19 shows Jesus and his disciples having a meal together.
If you were at the table with Jesus, what would you like to ask him?

The Last Supper

Jesus sat at the table with his disciples. He
said, "I want to share this supper with you."

Then Jesus took the bread. He blessed it
and broke it. He gave it to them and said,
"This is my body which will be given for
you. Do this in memory of me."

After the meal he took a cup of wine. He said,
"This is my blood. It is given for you."

adapted from Luke 22:14–20

Thank You, God

Write a thank-you note
inside the gift box,
thanking God for the
gift of his Son.

Reading God's Word

Jesus sacrificed himself for our sins. He is with God forever.

adapted from Hebrews 10:12

Name _____ Date _____

Art Print 20 shows Jesus hanging on the cross. Do you know someone who wears a cross on a necklace? What do you think that means?

Lent and Holy Week

Lent begins with Ash Wednesday. Ashes are put on our foreheads. The ashes are a sign that we are sorry for our sins.

The last week of Lent is Holy Week. It is a special time for remembering. We remember all that happened leading to Jesus' Death and Resurrection.

On Palm Sunday we remember Jesus' entrance into Jerusalem. On Holy Thursday we recall how Jesus gave himself to us in the Eucharist. On Good Friday we remember how Jesus suffered and died. At the vigil Mass on Holy Saturday, we celebrate Jesus' Resurrection.

Jesus died for our sins so that we could live a new life. With Jesus' help we can learn to care for others as Jesus did.

About Lent

Write a word from the word box to finish each sentence.

> change   Lent   remember   prepare

1. Lent is a time to _____ what Jesus has done for us.

2. During Lent we _____ for Easter.

3. The last week of _____ begins with Palm Sunday.

4. During Lent we _____ our ways to follow Jesus.

Name _____ Date _____

Art Print 21 shows Jesus' plan for true happiness that we call the Beatitudes. How does following Jesus make you happy?

Reaching Out to Others

Many people came to hear Jesus. He talked to them about ways to live a happy life. He gave them a plan to follow. This plan is called the **Beatitudes.** The Beatitudes help us to live more like Jesus.

One Beatitude teaches us to reach out to others. We do this by sharing, helping, and showing kindness in our words and actions.

Jesus said, "Blessed are those who are kind to others. They shall have kindness shown to them."

adapted from Matthew 5:7

Blessed Are the Kind

Write about a time you showed kindness. Write about a time someone was kind to you.

_____

_____

_____

_____

Link to Liturgy

At the end of Mass, we are blessed and sent forth. The priest or deacon says, "Go forth, the Mass is ended." We say, "Thanks be to God."

Name _____ Date _____

Art Print 22 shows Moses receiving the Ten Commandments from God. How can you show that you know the commandments?

Follow God's Laws

Moses was a great leader of the Jewish people. He led them to freedom. He reminded them why it was important to do what God wanted.

Moses said, "Good things will happen if you obey the Ten Commandments. Love God and follow his laws. Then you will be blessed."

"You can also choose not to follow God. Then you will not be blessed. The choice is yours to make."

adapted from Deuteronomy 30:16–18

Choose God

Read each sentence. One word is scrambled.
Draw a line from the sentence to the unscrambled word.

1. **osMse** was a great leader. ●   ● **a.** freedom

2. Moses led the people to **dmerfeo**. ●   ● **b.** Commandments

3. Obey the **manCommnetsd**. ●   ● **c.** laws

4. Choose to follow God's **wlsa**. ●   ● **d.** Moses

Reading God's Word

Jesus said, "I am the way, the truth, and the life."

adapted from John 14:6

Name _____   Date _____

Art Print 23 shows friends playing and bringing joy to their neighborhood. How are you a good neighbor where you live?

Love Your Neighbor

Jesus often spoke about loving one another. He teaches us that all people are our neighbors and that we should love them as we do ourselves.

Jesus' teachings tell us, "If you see a neighbor who needs help, do not close your heart to this person. Your love is not to be just words you say. Love must be something that you do."

adapted from 1 John 3:17–18

Love in Action

Jesus teaches us to love others as we love ourselves. Write down some ways you show love in your life.

Name people you love.	**Name things you love.**
_____	_____
_____	_____
_____	_____
What do you say to show love?	**What do you do to show love?**
_____	_____
_____	_____
_____	_____

Name _____ Date _____

Art Print 24 shows a mother teaching her son to walk.
How do we learn to help one another?

Respect Others

God wants us to treat everyone with
love and kindness. He teaches us that
we will be happy if we show respect
for others and their feelings.

We can show respect by
- ► living in peace with others.
- ► saying kind things about one another.
- ► returning things we borrow.

Keeping the Peace

Write ways that you can be a peacemaker by showing respect.

I show respect to my family when I _____

_____ .

I show respect to friends and neighbors when I _____

_____ .

Link to Liturgy

At Mass the sign of peace is one way we show respect
for others.

Name _____ Date _____

Art Print 25 shows a bouquet of lilies. If you could give the risen Jesus a bouquet of flowers, what kind would you give? Why?

We Celebrate Easter

Easter is the most joyful season of the Church year. On Easter Sunday we celebrate Jesus' Resurrection from the dead. During the Easter season, we also remember Jesus' Ascension into Heaven. Jesus Christ is there with God the Father.

The Easter Season lasts 50 days. It ends on Pentecost Sunday. On that day the Holy Spirit came to the disciples. Then they went out to tell the world about Jesus.

Jesus brings us all the gift of Salvation. We can live in peace, knowing that we have been saved.

Alleluia

Write an Easter prayer. End with *Alleluia.*

_____

_____

_____

_____

_____

Glossary

A

absolution the forgiveness of God. In the Sacrament of Penance and Reconciliation, we say that we are sorry for our sins. Then the priest offers us God's absolution. [absolución]

Advent the four weeks before Christmas. It is a time of joyful preparation for the celebration of Jesus' birth. [Adviento]

Alleluia a prayer of praise to God. It is usually sung before the Gospel Reading at Mass. [Aleluya]

All Saints Day November 1, the day on which the Church honors all who have died and now live with God as saints in Heaven. These saints include all those who have been declared saints by the Church and many others known only to God. [Día de Todos los Santos]

All Souls Day November 2, the day on which the Church remembers all who have died as friends of God. We pray that they may rest in peace. [Día de los Fieles Difuntos]

altar the table in the church on which the priest celebrates Mass. On this table the bread and wine are offered to God and become the Body and Blood of Jesus Christ. [altar]

ambo a platform from which a person reads the Word of God during Mass [ambón]

Amen the last word in any prayer that we pray. *Amen* means "This is true." We pray "Amen" to show that we really mean the words we have just said. [Amén]

angel a messenger from God [ángel]

Ash Wednesday the first day of Lent. We receive ashes on our foreheads on this day to remind us to show sorrow for the choices we make that hurt our friendships with God and with others. [Miércoles de Ceniza]

B

Baptism the first of the three sacraments by which we become members of the Church. Baptism frees us from Original Sin and gives us new life in Jesus Christ through the Holy Spirit. [Bautismo]

Beatitudes the eight ways we can behave in order to lead a Christian life. Jesus explains that if we live according to the Beatitudes, we are living as his followers. [Bienaventuranzas]

Bible the written story of God's promise to care for us, especially through his Son, Jesus [Biblia]

bishop a leader in the Church. Bishops teach us what God is asking of us as followers of Jesus today. [obispo]

Blessed Sacrament the Eucharist that has been consecrated by the priest at Mass. It is kept in the tabernacle to adore and to be taken to those who are sick. [Santísimo Sacramento]

Body and Blood of Christ the Bread and Wine that has been consecrated by the priest at Mass [Cuerpo y Sangre de Cristo]

Bread of Life a title for Jesus that tells us he is the Bread, or food, for the faithful [pan de vida]

C

catholic a word that means "all over the world." The Church is catholic because Jesus gave the Church to the whole world. [católico]

celebrant a bishop or priest who leads the people in praying the Mass [celebrante]

celebrate to praise and worship God in a special way [celebrar]

chasuble the visible liturgical vestment worn by the bishop or priest at Mass. The newly ordained priest receives a chasuble as part of the ordination ritual. [casulla]

Christ a title, like *Messiah*, that means "anointed with oil." It is the name given to Jesus after the Resurrection. [Cristo]

Christian the name given to people who want to live as Jesus taught us to live [cristiano]

Christmas the day on which we celebrate the birth of Jesus (December 25) [Navidad]

Church the name given to the followers of Christ all over the world. Spelled with a small *c*, *church* is the name of the building in which we gather to pray to God. [Iglesia]

commandment a rule that tells us how to live as God wants us to live [mandamiento]

confession the act of telling our sins to a priest in the Sacrament of Penance and Reconciliation [confesión]

Confirmation the sacrament that completes the grace we receive in Baptism [Confirmación]

conscience the inner voice that helps each of us know what God wants us to do [conciencia]

consecration the making of a thing or person to be special to God through prayer. At Mass the words of the priest are a consecration of the bread and wine. This makes them the Body and Blood of Jesus Christ. [consagración]

contrition the sadness we feel when we know that we have sinned [contrición]

creation everything that God has made. God said that all of creation is good. [creación]

Creator God, who made everything that is [Creador]

crosier the staff carried by a bishop. This staff shows that the bishop cares for us in the same way that a shepherd cares for his sheep. [báculo]

D

deacon a man who accepts God's call to serve the Church. Deacons help the bishop and priests in the work of the Church. [diácono]

disciple a person who is a follower of Jesus and tries to live as he did [discípulo]

E

Easter the celebration of the bodily raising of Jesus Christ from the dead. Easter is the most important Christian feast. [Pascua]

Emmanuel a name that means "God with us." It is a name given to Jesus. [Emanuel]

eternal life living happily with God in Heaven after we die [vida eterna]

Eucharist the sacrament in which we give thanks to God for giving us Jesus Christ [Eucaristía]

Evangelists the four men credited with writing the Gospels of Matthew, Mark, Luke, and John [evangelista]

examination of conscience thinking about what we have said or done that may have hurt our friendship with God or with others [examen de conciencia]

F

faith a gift of God. Faith helps us to believe in God and live as he wants us to live. [fe]

forgiveness the act of being kind to people who have hurt us but then have said that they are sorry. God always forgives us when we say that we are sorry. We forgive others the way God forgives us. [perdón]

Fruits of the Holy Spirit the ways in which we act because God is alive in us [frutos del Espíritu Santo]

G

genuflect to show respect in church by touching a knee to the ground, especially in front of the tabernacle [genuflexión, hacer la]

gestures the movements we make, such as the Sign of the Cross or bowing, to show our reverence during prayer [gestos]

God the Father, Son, and Holy Spirit. God created us, saves us, and lives in us. [Dios]

godparent a witness to Baptism. A godparent helps the baptized person to live as a follower of Jesus. [padrino/madrina de Bautismo]

grace the gift of God given to us without our earning it. Sanctifying grace fills us with God's life and makes us his friends. [gracia]

Great Commandment Jesus' important teaching that we are to love both God and other people [Mandamiento Mayor, el]

guardian angel the angel who has been appointed to help a person grow close to God [ángel de la guarda]

H

Heaven the life with God that is full of happiness and never ends [cielo]

holy showing the kind of life we live when we cooperate with the grace of God [santa]

Holy Communion the consecrated Bread and Wine that we receive at Mass, which is the Body and Blood of Jesus Christ [Sagrada Comunión]

Holy Days of Obligation those days other than Sundays on which we celebrate the great things God has done for us through Jesus Christ [días de precepto]

Holy Family the family made up of Jesus; his mother, Mary; and his foster father, Joseph [Sagrada Familia]

Holy Spirit the third Person of the Trinity, who comes to us in Baptism and fills us with God's life [Espíritu Santo]

holy water water that has been blessed. It is used to remind us of our Baptism. [agua bendita]

Holy Week the week that celebrates the events of Jesus' giving us the Eucharist, his suffering, Death, and Resurrection [Semana Santa]

Homily an explanation of God's Word. The Homily explains the Word of God that we hear in the Bible readings at church. [homilía]

honor giving to God or a person the respect that they are owed [honrar]

hope the trust that God will always be with us. We also trust that he will make us happy now and help us to live in a way that keeps us with him forever. [esperanza]

J

Jesus the Son of God, who was born of the Virgin Mary, died, was raised from the dead, ascended into Heaven, and saves us so that we can live with God forever [Jesús]

Joseph the foster father of Jesus, who was engaged to Mary when the angel announced that Mary would have a child through the power of the Holy Spirit [José]

K

Kingdom of God God's rule over us. We experience the Kingdom of God in part now. We will experience it fully in Heaven. [reino de Dios]

L

Last Supper the last meal Jesus ate with his disciples on the night before he died. Every Mass is a remembrance of that last meal. [Última Cena]

Lectionary for Mass the book from which the stories from the Bible are read at Mass [Leccionario]

Lent six weeks during which we prepare to celebrate, with special prayers and actions, the rising of Jesus from the dead at Easter. Jesus rose from the dead to save us. [Cuaresma]

Light of the World a name that helps us see that Jesus is the light that leads us to the Father [luz del mundo]

liturgy the public prayer of the Church that celebrates the wonderful things God has done for us in Jesus Christ [liturgia]

Liturgy of the Eucharist a main part of the Mass in which the bread and wine are consecrated and become the Body and Blood of Jesus Christ. We receive the Body and Blood of Jesus Christ in Holy Communion. [Liturgia de la Eucaristía]

Liturgy of the Word a main part of the Mass in which we listen to God's Word from the Bible. [Liturgia de la Palabra]

liturgical year the calendar that tells us when to celebrate the feasts of Jesus' birth, life, Death, Resurrection, and Ascension [año litúrgico]

M

Magnificat Mary's song of praise to God. She praises him for the great things he has done for her and for his plans for us through Jesus. [Magníficat]

Mary the mother of Jesus. She is "full of grace" because God chose her to be Jesus' mother. [María]

Mass our most important means of praying to God. At Mass we listen to God's Word, the Bible. The bread and wine are consecrated and become the Body and Blood of Jesus Christ. [misa]

Messiah a title, like *Christ,* that means "anointed with oil." *Messiah* also means "Savior." [Mesías]

ministry the service, or work, done for others. Ministry is done by bishops, priests, and deacons in the celebration of the sacraments. All those baptized are called to different kinds of ministry in the liturgy and in serving the needs of others. [ministerio]

miracle the healing of a person, or an occasion when nature is controlled because of God's action [milagro]

moral choice a choice to do what is right. We make moral choices because they help us grow closer to God. [opción moral]

mortal sin a serious choice to turn away from God [pecado mortal]

N

Nativity scene a picture or crèche that shows Jesus, Mary, and Joseph in the stable after the birth of Jesus as described in the Gospels of Matthew and Luke [escena de la Natividad del Señor]

neighbor for a Christian, every other person, as each person is made in God's image [prójimo]

New Testament the story of Jesus and the early Church [Nuevo Testamento]

O

obey to follow the teachings given by God or by someone who has the right to direct us [obedecer]

Old Testament the story of God's plan for Salvation before the birth of Jesus [Antiguo Testamento]

Ordinary Time the longest liturgical season of the Church. It is divided into two periods—one after the Christmas season and one after Pentecost. [Tiempo Ordinario]

Original Sin the result of the sin of Adam and Eve. They disobeyed God and chose to follow their own will rather than God's will. [pecado original]

P

parable one of the simple stories that Jesus told to show us what God wants for the world [parábola]

parish a community of believers in Jesus Christ who meet regularly to worship God together [parroquia]

peacemaker a person who teaches us to be respectful in our words and actions toward one another [paz, los que trabajar por la]

penance the turning away from sin so that we can live as God wants us to live (*See* Sacrament of Penance and Reconciliation.) [penitencia]

Pentecost the 50th day after Jesus was raised from the dead. On this day the Holy Spirit was sent from Heaven, and the Church was born. [Pentecostés]

petition a request we make to God, asking for what we need since we know that he created us and wants to give us what we need [petición]

pope the bishop of Rome, successor of Saint Peter, and leader of the Roman Catholic Church [Papa]

praise our telling of the happiness we feel simply because God is so good [alabanza]

prayer our talking to God and listening to him in our hearts [oración]

priest a man who accepts God's special call to serve the Church. Priests guide the Church and lead it in the celebration of the sacraments. [sacerdote]

R

reconciliation making friends again after a friendship has been broken by some action or lack of action. In the Sacrament of Penance and Reconciliation, we are reconciled with God, the Church, and others. [Reconciliación]

Resurrection the bodily raising of Jesus Christ from the dead on the third day after he died on the cross [Resurrección]

rite the special form followed in celebrating each sacrament [rito]

S

sacrament the way in which God enters our life. Through simple objects such as water, oil, and bread, Jesus continues to bless us. [sacramento]

Sacrament of Penance and Reconciliation the sacrament in which we celebrate God's forgiveness of our sins when we say to the priest that we are sorry for them [sacramento de la Penitencia y de la Reconciliación]

Sacraments of Initiation the sacraments that make us members of God's Church. They are Baptism, Confirmation, and the Eucharist. [sacramentos de iniciación]

Sacrifice of the Mass remembering the sacrifice of Jesus on the cross. We remember Jesus' sacrifice every time we celebrate Mass. [Sacrificio de la misa]

saint a holy person who has died as a true friend of God and now lives with God forever [santo]

Savior Jesus, the Son of God, who became man to make us friends with God again. *Jesus* means "God saves." [Salvador]

seal of confession refers to the fact that the priest must keep absolutely secret the sins that are confessed to him in the Sacrament of Penance and Reconciliation [sigilo sacramental]

Sign of Peace the part of the Mass in which we offer a gesture of peace to one another as we prepare to receive Holy Communion [rito de la paz]

sin a choice we make that hurts our friendships with God and with other people [pecado]

Son of God the name given to Jesus that reveals his special relationship to God the Father [Hijo de Dios]

T

tabernacle the container in which the Blessed Sacrament is kept so that Holy Communion can be taken to those who are sick [sagrario]

Temple the Temple in Jerusalem, the most important place where the Jewish people came to pray. They believed that this was the place where they could be closest to God. Jesus often came to pray in the Temple. [Templo, judío]

temptation a thought or feeling that can lead us to disobey God. Temptation can come either from outside us or inside us. [tentación]

Ten Commandments the ten rules that God gave to Moses. The Ten Commandments sum up God's law and show us how to live as his children. [Diez Mandamientos]

transubstantiation when the bread and wine become the Body and Blood of Jesus Christ [transubstanciación]

trespasses acts that harm others [ofensas]

Trinity the mystery of one God existing in three Persons: the Father, the Son, and the Holy Spirit [Trinidad]

V

venial sin a choice we make that weakens our relationships with God or with other people [pecado venial]

Index

A

absolution, 76, 215, 261
Act of Contrition, 72, 78, 190, 215
act of kindness, 215
Adam, 65
Advent, 27, 57–60, 90, 152, 153–56, 244, 261
Advent wreath, 155
All Saints Day, 152, 177–80, 209, 261
All Souls Day, 261
Alleluia, 204, 259, 261
altar, 112, 211, 261
altar server, 106, 210
ambo, 106, 210, 261
Amen, 208, 215, 261
angel, 170, 262
Anne, Saint, 31, 32
Anointing of the Sick, Sacrament of the, 200
Apostles' Creed, 193, 196
Ascension, 209, 259
Ash Wednesday, 117, 119, 254, 262

B

banquet, parable of the, 242
Baptism, Sacrament of, 17, 20, 29, 65, 94, 96, 97, 98, 149, 198, 262
Beatitudes, 128, 137, 139, 140, 218, 255 262
Bible, 262. *See also* Gospels
   Book of Psalms, 54
   knowing and praying our faith, 184–85
   in Mass, 185
bishop, 47, 262
Blessed Sacrament, the 11, 262
Blessing, Final, 207
Body and Blood of Christ, 28, 95, 112, 199, 208, 253, 262
Bread of Life, 28, 29, 30, 263

C

calendar
   liturgical, 27, 151
   Ordinary Time, 27
cantor, 211
caring for creation, 5, 220
caring for others, 23, 40, 43, 48, 220
catholic, 263
Catholic Church. *See* Church, the
celebrant, 263
celebrate, 263
chalice, 211
chastity, 219
chasuble, 30, 211, 239, 263
children, Jesus loves, 161, 178
Christ, 263. *See also* Jesus
Christian, 263
Christmas, 27, 87–90, 152, 157–60, 249, 263
Church, the, 136, 263
   church, as building, 263
   Jesus loves, 99–104
   leaders of, 46, 250
   Mary as Mother of, 248
   members of, 251
   Ordinary Time, 27
Collect Prayer, 203
commandment, 34–35, 264.
      See also Commandments, Ten
   Great Commandment, 136, 217, 266
   new commandment, 217
Commandments, Ten, 34–35, 216, 256, 274
Communion of Saints, 178
Communion Rite, 207.
      See also The Order of Mass
community, 220
community of believers, 142
Concluding Rites, 207.
      See also The Order of Mass

Acknowledgments

Excerpts from the *New American Bible with Revised New Testament and Psalms.* Copyright © 1991, 1986, 1970 Confraternity of Christian Doctrine, Inc., Washington, DC. Used with permission. All rights reserved. No part of the *New American Bible* may be reprinted without permission in writing from the copyright holder.

The English translation of the Act of Contrition from *Rite of Penance* © 1974, International Commission on English in the Liturgy Corporation (ICEL); the English translation of the Prayer to the Holy Spirit and *Salve, Regina* from *A Book of Prayers* © 1982, ICEL; the English translation of Prayer Before Meals and Prayer After Meals from *Book of Blessings* © 1988; the English translation of the Apostles' Creed from *The Roman Missal* © 2010, ICEL. All rights reserved.

For more information related to the English translation of the *Roman Missal, Third Edition*, see www.loyolapress.com/romanmissal.

Loyola Press has made every effort to locate the copyright holders for the cited works used in this publication and to make full acknowledgment for their use. In the case of any omissions, the publisher will be pleased to make suitable acknowledgments in future editions.

Art and Photography

When there is more than one picture on a page, positions are abbreviated as follows: (t) top, (c) center, (b) bottom, (l) left, (r) right, (bg) background, (bd) border.

Photos and illustrations not acknowledged are either owned by Loyola Press or from royalty-free sources including but not limited to Alamy, Corbis/Veer, Getty Images, Jupiterimages, PunchStock, Thinkstock, and Wikipedia Commons. Loyola Press has made every effort to locate the copyright holders for the cited works used in this publication and to make full acknowledgment for their use. In the case of any omissions, the publisher will be pleased to make suitable acknowledgments in future editions.

Frontmatter: i Rafael Lopez. **iii** Clockwise from top, (a) Mia Basile. **iii**(b) Julie Downing. **iii** (c) ©iStockphoto.com/jusant. **iii**(d) Stockbyte/Thinkstock. **iii**(e) Hemera/Thinkstock. **iii**(f) Joy Allen. **iii**(g) Polka Dot Images/Thinkstock. **iv** Clockwise from top, (a) iStockphoto/Thinkstock. **iv**(b) ©iStockphoto.com/agalma. **iv**(c) ©iStockphoto.com/JohnnyGreig. **iv**(d) Joy Allen. **iv**(e) ©iStockphoto.com/Kativ.

©iStockphoto.com: 1(t) hougaardmalan. **3** FDS111. **4**(b) jonya. **5**(t) arlindo71. **5**(br) spxChrome. **6** Mike_Kiev. **7**(t) archives. **7**(bl) birdseye. **7**(br) contour99. **8**(t) Pixlmaker. **8**(c) monkeybusinessimages. **8**(b) askhamdesign. **10** mammuth. **16**(t) OBXbchcmbr. **16**(b) pakagallardo. **17**(t) Alina555. **18** aldomurillo. **21** monkeybusinessimages. **23**(c) Yarinca. **23**(b) 13spoon. **28**(bc) aantozak. **29**(b) jusant. **35** Kativ. **37**(l) w-ings. **37**(br) stockhlm. **38**(b) aldomurillo. **41**(b) CraigRJD. **43**(tl) mstay. **43**(tr) o-che. **43**(b) mstay. **46**(tr) Barcin. **46**(b) Pierdelune. **48** juanestey. **49**(tl) mstay. **49**(cl) Andy445. **49**(cr) toddtaulman. **49**(cb) isgaby. **50**(b) sjlocke. **51** diephosi. **53**(br) Neustockimages. **56**(t) BCWH. **56**(b) Liliboas. **58** jusant. **59**(tl) T_Lykova. **59**(tr) grandaded. **59**(b) AYImages. **61**(t) absolutely_frenchy. **62**(r) bibikoff. **64**(cl) jabejon. **68**(br) mm88. **71**(cl) nicolesy. **71**(cr) nicolesy. **71**(b) jusant. **75** LindaYolanda. **79**(tl) ArtisticCaptures. **79**(tr) draco77. **79**(b) STEVECOLEccs. **80**(b) aldomurillo. **85**(bc) Andyd. **85**(b) blufox51. **87**(t) lenta. **87**(b) mmac72. **88–89**(b) craftvision. **89**(t) MarkM73. **93** RichVintage. **94**(t) choja. **94–95**(b) h2o_color. **94**(bc) kentarcajuan. **95**(tl) agalma. **99** Likhitha. **103** mstay. **104**(t) ArtisticCaptures. **111** kate_sept2004. **114** abalcazar. **118**(t) ManoAfrica. **118–119**(b) ooyoo. **120**(t) duckycards. **127**(t, b) mitza. **128** phillipspears. **131** arekmalang. **134**(t) ettone. **134**(b) Maica. **139**(c) Cybernesco. **140** RedBarnStudio. **143**(b) h2o_color. **143**(bc) tentan. **145**(t) exi5. **145**(bl) Favna. **145**(br) paperteacup. **146**(t) paulaphoto. **147**(t) cobalt. **147**(b) Kativ. **149**(t) duckycards. **154**(bl) Hogie. **158**(b) ultra_generic. **163**(tc) bo1982. **163**(tr) alptraum. **163**(bl) bo1982. **163**(bc) bbostjan. **165**(t) Elenathewise. **169**(c) BCWH. **171**(b) golovorez. **175**(ct) JohnnyGreig. **175**(cb) PicturePartners. **175**(br) jane. **180** Jbryson. **181** Clockwise from top, (a) lucato. **181**(e) lushik. **182–183**(b) CEFutcher. **184**(b) digitalskillet. **185**(c) Terrie L. Zeller/Shutterstock.com. **186**(t) CraigRJD. **189**(br) sugapopcandy. **205**(t) Mixmike. **205**(b) CEFutcher. **216**(b) iStockphoto. **216–217**(bg) CEFutcher. **220–221**(b) Liliboas. **220–221**(b) gbh007. **221**(c) ranplett. **227**(t) EricVega. **233**(t) jaminwell. **245** FreeTransform. **249**(t) ultra_generic. **251** Art-Y.

Thinkstock: 12 Jupiterimages/Creatas. **19** iStockphoto. **24** Ryan McVay/Lifesize. **26**(b) Jupiterimages/Pixland. **27**(t) iStockphoto. **28**(c) Stockbyte. **28**(bl) Polka Dot Images/Polka Dot. **28**(br) iStockphoto. **30** Jenny Acheson/Stockbyte. **33**(t) Jupiterimages/Brand X Pictures. **36** Jupiterimages/Pixland. **42**(b) iStockphoto. **44**(bl) iStockphoto. **44**(br) iStockphoto. **57**(t) iStockphoto. **60**(b) Stockbyte. **63** Jupiterimages/Comstock. **64**(cr) Jupiterimages/Photos.com. **64**(b) iStockphoto. **65**(l) John Foxx/Stockbyte. **65**(cl,b) Hemera. **68**(bl) Jupiterimages/Creatas. **72** iStockphoto. **73** Jupiterimages/liquidlibrary. **74** Creatas Images/Creatas. **76–77**(c) Ryan McVay/Photodisc. **76–77**(b) Hemera Technologies/AbleStock.com. **77**(bl) iStockphoto. **80**(t) iStockphoto. **81** Hemera. **86**(b) Comstock Images/Comstock. **102** Jupiterimages/Polka Dot. **104**(bl) Comstock Images/Cornstock. **104**(br) iStockphoto. **105** Jupiterimages/Pixland. **108** Jupiterimages/Polka Dot. **116**(b) David Sacks/Lifesize. **117**(t) iStockphoto. **120**(b) Jupiterimages/Brand X Pictures. **122**(b) Jupiterimages/Comstock. **126** Ciaran Griffin/Stockbyte. **129**(c) Ciaran Griffin/iStockbyte. **130**(t) Ciaran Griffin/iStockbyte. **132** iStockphoto. **133**(t) Jupiterimages/Photos.com. **136–137** ajaykampani/Thinkstock. **138**(t,b) iStockphoto. **138**(c) iStockphoto. **139**(t) iStockphoto. **141** BananaStock. **143**(t) Stockbyte. **143**(ct) iStockphoto. **144** Jupiterimages/Goodshoot. **146**(b) Jupiterimages/Polka Dot. **149**(b) iStockphoto. **150**(t) iStockphoto. **150**(b) Jupiterimages/Comstock. **152**(cb) Hemera Technologies/AbleStock.com. **154–155**(b) iStockphoto. **157**(t) iStockphoto. **159**(b) Jupiterimages/Comstock. **160**(b) Hemera. **163**(tl) Hemera. **163**(br) Jupiterimages/Brand X Pictures. **169**(tl, cr) iStockphoto. **171**(c) Hemera. **175**(t) Kraig Scarbinsky/Photodisc. **176** Stockbyte. **179**(t) Creatas Images/Creatas. **181**(b) iStockphoto. **183**(l) iStockphoto. **186–187**(b) Hemera. **188–189**(b) iStockphoto. **194**(t) iStockphoto. **194–195**(b) iStockphoto. **196**(b) iStockphoto. **206–207**(bd) Hemera. **212**(b) iStockphoto. **213**(l) iStockphoto. **213**(r) iStockphoto. **217**(t) Jack Hollingsworth/Digital Vision. **218**(b) Jupiterimages/liquidlibrary. **219** Hemera. **221**(tr) Hemera. **222–234** (music notes) iStockphoto.

Unit 1: 1(b) Ed Gazsi. **2**(t) Ed Gazsi. **2**(bl) Jupiterimages. **2**(br) Royalty-free image. **4**(t) The Crosiers/Gene Plaisted, OSC. **5**(bl) Jupiterimages. **9** Alloy/Veer. **11**(t) Phil Martin Photography. **11**(b) AgnusImages.com. **13** Peter Church. **14** Moonboard/Veer. **15** Ocean Photography/Veer. **17**(c) Fr. William Hart McNicols. **17**(b) AgnusImages.com. **20** Photos.com. **22** Peter Church. **23**(t) allOver photography/Alamy. **25** Joy Allen. **26**(t) The Crosiers/Gene Plaisted, OSC. **27**(b) Warlling Studios. **28**(t) Greg Kuepfer. **29**(t) Jill Arena.

Unit 2: 31(t) Blend Images/Veer. **31**(b) Ed Gazsi. **32**(t) Ed Gazsi. **32**(b) Peter Church. **34**(b) Ron Chapple Stock/Alamy. **37**(tr) Peter Church. **37**(bc) Peter Church. **38**(t) Christina Balit. **39** Corbis Photography/Veer. **40** Peter Church. **41**(t) The Crosiers/Gene Plaisted, OSC. **44**(t) Jupiterimages. **45** Ocean Photography/Veer. **46**(tl) www.picturesongold.com/Loyola Press Photography. **46**(c) Andia/Alamy. **47**(t) Robert Harding Picture Library Ltd/Alamy. **47**(c) The Crosiers/Gene Plaisted, OSC. **47**(b) Liam White/Alamy. **49**(tr) Ed Gazsi. **49**(b) Br. Steve Erspamer. **50**(t) Lebrecht Music and Arts Photo Library/Alamy. **52**(t,b) Peter Church. **53**(l) Phil Martin Photography. **53**(tr) Custom Medical Stock Photo/Alamy. **53**(c) Ohad Reinhartz/Alamy. **54** Arctic Images/Alamy. **55** Olwyn Whelan. **57**(c) Alloy/Veer. **57**(b) Thomas Northcut/Photodisc/Jupiterimages. **60**(t) Kurt Adler.

Unit 3: 61(b) Ed Gazsi. **62**(l) Ed Gazsi. **62**(b) John Quinn SJ. **64**(t) Susan Tolonen. **65**(r) Julie Downing. **65**(cr) Robert Dant/Alamy. **66**(t) Julie Downing. **66**(b) Collage Photographer/Veer. **67** Julie Downing. **68**(t) Julie Downing. **69**(t) Ocean/Veer. **70**(t) Warling Studios **70**(b) Royalty-free image. **71**(t) Royalty-free image. **76**(t) Warling Studios. **77**(t) Phil Martin Photography. **78** RedChopsticks/Getty Images. **82–83**(b) Peter Church. **83**(t) Peter Church. **84** Warling Studios. **85**(t) The Crosiers/Gene Plaisted, OSC. **85**(r) The Crosiers/ Gene Plaisted, OSC. **86**(t) Loyola Press Photography. **87**(c) Nativity with Angels by Cathy Baxter (Contemporary Artist) Private Collection/ The Bridgeman Art Library. **90**(t) Roger Cope/Alamy. **90**(b) W. P. Wittman Limited.

Unit 4: 91(t) Phil Crean/Alamy. **91**(b) Ed Gazsi. **92**(t) W. P. Wittman Limited. **92**(b) Ed Gazsi. **94**(ct) Art Directors & TRIP/Alamy. **94**(cb) W. P. Wittman Limited. **95**(tr) Brian Warling Studios. **96** OJO Images Photography/Veer. **97** Susan Tolonen. **97**(b) Susan Tolonen. **98**(t) W. P. Wittman Limited. **98**(b) Jeff Greenberg/Alamy. **100** Joy Allen. **101**(t) The Crosiers/Gene Plaisted, OSC. **101**(bl) W. P. Wittman Limited. **101**(br) W. P. Wittman Limited. **106**(t) M.T.M. Images/ Alamy. **106**(b) W. P. Wittman Limited. **107** W. P. Wittman Limited. **109**(t) Harnett/Hanzon/Photodisc/Getty Images. **109**(b) W. P. Wittman Limited. **110**(t) W. P. Wittman Limited. **110**(b) W. P. Wittman Limited. **112**(t) W. P. Wittman Limited. **112**(b) W. P. Wittman Limited. **113** M.T.M. Images/Alamy. **115** Mia Basile McGloin. **116**(t) Kasey Hund. **117**(b) W. P. Wittman Limited. **119**(t) Kim Karpeles/Alamy.

Unit 5: 121(t) Vanni Archive/Corbis. **121**(b) Ed Gazsi. **122**(t) Ed Gazsi. **123** Cultura Photography/Veer. **124–125** Peter Church. **127**(cl, cr) Joy Allen. **129**(t) Fancy Photography/Veer. **130**(bl) The Crosiers/Gene Plaisted, OSC. **130**(br) W.P. Wittman Limited. **133**(b) The Crosiers/ Gene Plaisted, OSC. **134**(b) Big Cheese Photo LLC/Alamy. **135** Somos Photography/Veer. **136–137** Peter Church. **139**(b) Ed Gazsi. **142** Peter Church. **143**(cb) Agencja FREE/Alamy. **148** *Resurrection*, Raffaellino del Garbo/Galleria dell' Accademia, Florence, Italy/The Bridgeman Art Library International.

Seasonal Sessions: 151 Susan Tolonen. **152**(t) Zvonimir Atletic/ Shutterstock.com. **152**(ct) stevanovic.igor/Shutterstock.com. **152**(b) Royalty-free image. **153**(t) Zvonimir Atletic/Shutterstock. com. **153**(b) Warling Studios. **154**(t) Profimedia International s.r.o./ Alamy. **154**(br) Jupiterimages. **155** Kristina Swarner. **156** Blend Images/ Alamy. **157**(b) Peter Church. **158**(t) Peter Church. **159**(t) Greg Kuepfer. **160**(t) Royalty-free image. **161** Peter Church. **162** Peter Church. **164** Warling Studios. **165**(b) Peter Church. **166** Peter Church. **168** Tetra Images/Alamy. **169**(tr) Blend Images/Alamy. **169**(b) Jupiterimages. **170** Julie Downing. **171**(t) Anna Leplar. **172** Paul Simcock/Corbis. **173**(t) AgnusImages.com. **173**(b) Peter Church. **174** Peter Church. **175**(bl) ColonialArts.com. **177**(t) Warling Studios. **177**(b) Robert Young/Shutterstock.com. **178**(t) The Crosiers/Gene Plaisted, OSC. **178**(c) AgnusImages.com. **178**(b) Warling Studios. **179**(b) Jupiterimages.

Endmatter: 181(c) Jupiterimages. **181**(d) Zvonimir Atletic/Shutterstock. com. **183**(r) Photos.com. **184**(t) Shutterstock.com. **185**(t) W. P. Wittman Limited. **185**(b) Royalty-free image. **186**(c) Design Pics Inc./Alamy. **188**(t) Ocean/Corbis. **190** Stephen Flint/Alamy. **191** Blend Images/ Alamy. **192**(t) Royalty-free image. **192–193**(b) Corey Hochachka/ Alloy Photography/Veer. **193**(t) Jupiterimages. **195**(t) Helga Esteb/ Shutterstock.com. **195**(c) Jeff Haynes/AFP/Getty Images. **196**(t) Warling Studios. **197** Greg Kuepfer. **198**(t) Susan Tolonen. **198**(b) W. P. Wittman Limited. **199**(t) W. P. Wittman Limited. **199**(c) W. P. Wittman Limited. **199**(b) Susan Tolonen. **200**(t) Warling Studios. **200**(b) Susan Tolonen. **201**(t) The Crosiers/Gene Plaisted, OSC. **201**(b) Digital Vision/Getty Images. **202** W. P. Wittman Limited. **203**(t) Jupiterimages. **203**(b) Royalty-free image. **204**(t) W. P. Wittman Limited. **204**(b) Flancer/Alamy. **206**(t) Zvonimir Atletic/iStockphoto. com. **206**(b) Warling Studios. **207**(t) Warling Studios. **207**(b) Zvonimir Atletic/Shutterstock.com. **208**(t) Zvonimir Atletic/Shutterstock.com. **208–209**(b) Susan Tolonen. **210**(t) Warling Studios. **210–211**(b) Phyllis Pollema-Cahill. **211**(tl) W. P. Wittman Limited. **211**(tc) Warling Studios. **211**(tr) Phil Martin Photography. **212**(t) Royalty-free image. **214**(t) Warling Studios. **214**(c) Warling Studios. **214**(b) W. P. Wittman Limited. **215** Warling Studios. **218**(t) Elizabeth Wang/Radiant Light/ The Bridgeman Art Library International. **220**(t) Warling Studios. **220**(c) Royalty-free image. **221**(tl) Royalty-free image. **222**(t) AWEN art studio/Shutterstock.com. **223**(t) Roman Sigaev/Shutterstock.com. **223**(b) Image Source/Alamy. **224** italianestro/Shutterstock.com.

225(t) Royalty-free image. **226**(br) The Crosiers/Gene Plaisted, OSC. **228**(b) Alloy Photography/Veer. **229**(t) Katelyn Franke. **230** Royalty- free image. **231**(t) Maria Dryfhout/Shutterstock.com. **231**(br) George Doyle/Stockbyte/Getty Images. **232**(bl) WoodyStock/Alamy. **234**(b) Ben Molyneux People/Alamy. **235** Jim Effler. **236** Peter Church. **237** Jupiterimages. **238** Inguna Irbe. **239** Greg Phillips. **240** Yoshi Miyake. **241** Peter Church. **242** Jupiterimages. **243** Yoshi Miyake. **244** Inguna Irbe. **246** Peter Church. **247** Greg Phillips. **249**(b) Yoshi Miyake. **250** Peter Church. **252** © The Crosiers/Gene Plaisted, OSC. **253** Tony Rothberg. **254** Jupiterimages. **255** Yoshi Miyake. **256** Peter Church.